주니어

고릴라 영문법

Junior Gorilla Grammar

level 1

KB019658

핵심만 반복
그리고 영작!

2,500여 개의 전국 중학교 기출 문제 및 교과서 완전 분석 후 반영

www.taborm.com

주니어 고릴라 영문법 Level 1 ｜ Junior Gorilla Grammar 1

저자　타보름 교재 개발팀
디자인　김경희
발행인　이선미
발행일　개정 5쇄 2022년 8월 5일
발행처　타보름 교육
홈페이지　www.taborm.com

주니어
고릴라 영문법
교재 소개

문법 공부를 위한 문법책이 아닙니다.

1회성 시험만을 위한 문법책이 아닙니다.

그것보다는 조금은 욕심을 냈습니다.

시행착오를 겪기 전에
반복할 수 있게 했습니다.

영어가 싫어지지 않을 만큼만
반복하게 했습니다.

자신감이 붙어 즐길 수 있게 될 만큼만
반복하게 했습니다.

교육 이론만 가지고 만든 교재가 아닙니다.

1년간 수업을 해보고
더하기 빼기를 한 후 나온 교재입니다.

- 타보름 교재 개발팀

타보름 대표 교재 한 눈에 보기

주니어 고릴라 영문법 Level 1,2,3

추천 대상 | 중등부

중등부의 탄탄한 기초와 흥미 유지를 위한
핵심 반복과 영작 연습!

정가   13,500원 (Level 1)
　　　　 14,200원 (Level 2, 3)

핵꿀잼 리딩 Level 1,2,3

추천 대상 | 중등부

사랑, 공포, 지식, 유머, 심리 테스트까지
독해 욕구 완전 풀가동!

정가   12,000원 (Level 1,2,3)

수능X고등내신 영문법 2400제

추천 대상 ｜ 고등부

문법 기초부터 심화까지 독해에

필수적인 문법만을 반복해서 연습

단원별로 제공되는 수능 기출예문을 통해

실적 감각도 상승!

정가　13,800원

교육부 지정 중고등 영단어 3000

추천 대상 ｜ 성인 및 중고등부

교육부가 지정한 필수 영단어를 포켓북으로!

랜덤 단어 무제한 테스트 생성기

무료제공으로 확실하게 암기한다

무제한 단어 테스트 생성기 무료제공

정가　6,800원

수능 절대평가 1등급 영단어 4000

추천 대상 ｜ 성인 및 고등부

최근 7개년의 수능 및 모의고사를 분석, 수능 영어

절대평가 유형 문제 풀이의 최중요 4,000단어

휴대가 간편한 B5 사이즈

무제한 단어 테스트 생성기 무료제공

정가　7,700원

unit 3 인칭대명사

인칭	격		주격	소유격	목적격	소유대명사
	수		(주어자리)	(명사수식)	(목적어자리)	
1인칭	단수		I	my	me	mine
	복수		we	our	us	ours
2인칭	단수		you	your	you	your
	복수		you	your	you	you
3인칭	단수	남성	he	his	him	h
		여성	she	her	her	
		중성	it	its	it	
	복수		they	their	them	

★ 용어설명
• 1인칭: '나(본인)'를 말한다.
• 2인칭: '너(상대방)'를 말한다.
• 3인칭: '나'와 '너'를 제외한 모든 것을 말한다.

• 단수: 한 개
• 복수: 둘 이상

주어	동사	목적어	해석
I	met	her.	나는 그
She	met	him.	고
He	met	us.	
We	met	them.	
They	met		

step 2
반복문제를 통한
깨달음 유도

...se 1

...어진 단어에 맞는 인칭대명사를

1. John → (you / he / they)

2. Mike and Sue → (she / they / I

3. My Friends → (he / she / they)

4. Jane's → (she / her / him)

5. My watch → (he / ours / mine)

6. A book → (it / they / you)

7. I and you → (they / herself / w

8. You and me → (them / us / its)

 Her pencil → (she / her / hers)

 ...r money → (we / us / the

step 1
깔끔하고
잡은 설명

rcise 2 ------------------------------

주어진 단어를 이용하여 영작하시오.

. 그녀는 예쁘지 않다. (pretty)
→

. 그는 매우 잘 생겼다. (handsome)
→

. 그들은 친절하다. (kind)
→

. 너는 혼자니? (alone)
→

. 나는 집에 있다. (home)

step 4

여러 단계에 걸친
테스트!

step 3

이해종결을 위한
영작!

Chapter Exercise

Chapter Exercise 1

다음 문장을 영작하세요.

1. 나는 영어를 말할 수 있다.
→

2. 나는 졸려서 잘 수 없다.
→

3. 네가 도와드릴까요?
→

4. 이 영화는 나에게 지루함이 들었습니다.
→

Exercise

Unit Exercise 1

괄호 안에 알맞은 표현을 고르고 해석하세요.

1. He never tells me (what /that) I want to hear fro

2. (Whether /If) she can speak Korean is uncertain

3. (That /Whether) your father is rich or not is not

4. I wonder (why /what) he can swim well.

5. This is (that /what) he wants to have.

6. She doesn't believe (that /why) I am a liar.

7. I think (that /when) this is a spoon.

8. (What /How) I have lived my life can affect his

주니어 고릴라 영문법의 학습 구성

Junior Gorilla Grammar Level 1

주니어
고릴라 영문법
목차

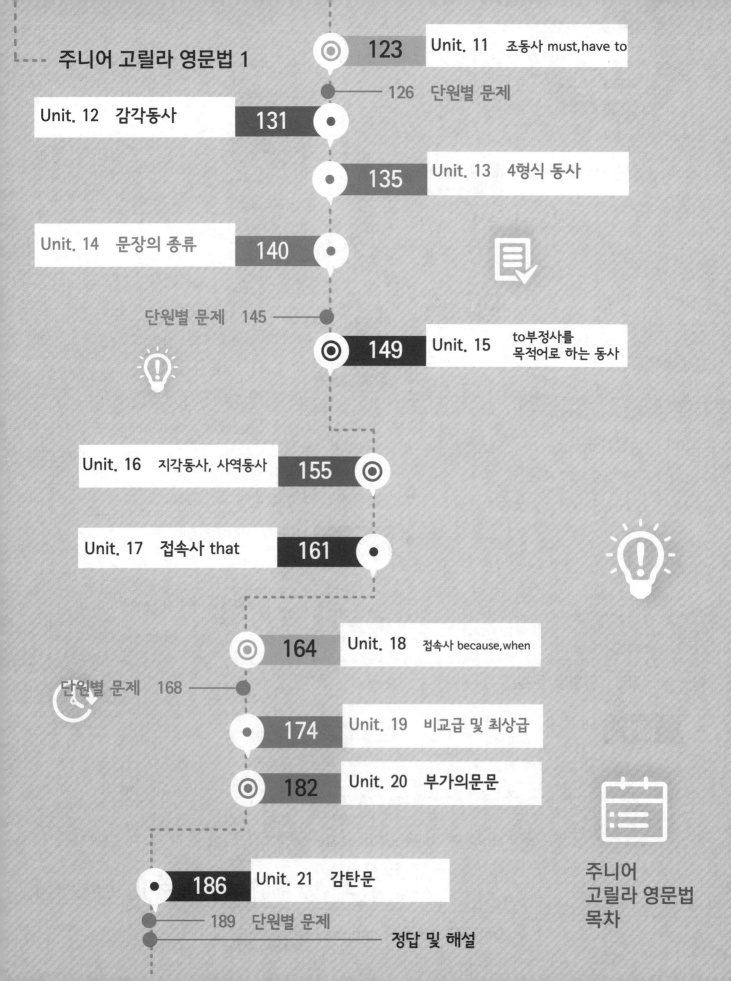

주니어
고릴라 영문법
목차

Unit 1   단어의 종류

- 명사
- 동사
- 형용사
- 부사

Gorilla Grammar

unit 1 　단어의 종류

1 　(대)명사

- 생물이나 무생물의 이름을 나타내는 말이다.

  (Ex: 주희, 서연, 책상, 도덕, 모래, 물 등)

- 대명사는 명사를 대신해 쓰는 말이다.

  (Ex: 그, 그녀, 그것, 그들 등)

2 　동사

- 주어의 동작이나 상태를 나타내는 말.

  (Ex: 자다, 놀다, 공부하다 등)

3 　형용사

- 문장에서 명사를 수식하거나 보어 자리에 들어간다.

  (Ex: 예쁜, 귀여운, 착한, 경건한 등) 　(활용: 예쁜 주희, 귀여운 서연 등)

4 　부사

- 형용사, 동사, 또 다른 부사, 문장전체의 수식을 담당한다.

  (Ex: 잘, 너무, 매우, 예쁘게, 귀엽게, 착하게 등) 　(활용: 너무 예쁜, 잘 잔다, 등)

- -

★ 문장의 형식은 동사에 달려있음

　(Ex: sleep-1형식, be동사-1,2형식, meet-3형식)

★ 동사로 시제와 태를 나타낸다.

　(Ex: 잔다, 잤다, 잘 것이다 등)

---- **Exercise 1** ---

다음 제시된 단어의 종류를 하나만 작성하세요.

1. 집 _____   6. 얼음 _____

2. 공부하다 _____   7. 매우 _____

3. 귀여운 _____   8. 돈 _____

4. 큰 _____   9. 사랑 _____

5. 크게 _____   10. 눕다 _____

---- **Exercise 1-1** ---

다음 제시된 단어의 종류를 하나만 작성하세요.

1. nice _____   6. pretty _____

2. sometimes _____   7. prettily _____

3. have _____   8. book _____

4. trip _____   9. pencil _____

5. travel _____   10. sleep _____

Unit 2 인칭대명사

Gorilla Grammar

unit 2   인칭대명사

인칭	격 수		주격 (주어자리)	소유격 (명사수식)	목적격 (목적어자리)	소유대명사
1인칭	단수		I	my	me	mine
	복수		we	our	us	ours
2인칭	단수		you	your	you	yours
	복수		you	your	you	yours
3인칭	단 수	남성	he	his	him	his
		여성	she	her	her	hers
		중성	it	its	it	x
	복수		they	their	them	theirs

- -

★ 용어설명

• 1인칭: '나(본인)'를 말한다.

• 2인칭: '너(상대방)'를 말한다.

• 3인칭: '나'와 '너'를 제외한 모든 것을 말한다.

• 단수: 한 개

• 복수: 둘 이상

주어	동사	목적어	해석	소유격	명사
I	met	her.	나는 그녀를 만났다.	my	car
She	met	him.	그녀는 그를 만났다.	her	car
He	met	us.	그는 우리를 만났다.	his	car
We	met	them.	우리는 그들을 만났다.	our	car
They	met	me.	그들은 나를 만났다.	their	car

---- **Exercise 1** --

다음 해석에 맞게 빈칸을 채우세요.

1._____don't like it. (그들은 그것을 좋아하지 않는다.)

2._____loves him. (그녀는 그를 사랑한다.)

3._____are so kind. (당신은 참 친절하다.)

4._____have a big house. (우리는 큰 집을 소유하고 있다.)

5._____doesn't have enough money. (그는 충분한 돈을 가지고 있지 않다.)

6._____can do it by myself. (나는 스스로 그것을 할 수 있다.)

7._____are so heavy. (그것들은 매우 무겁다.)

8._____is my favorite book. (그것은 내가 가장 좋아하는 책이다.)

9._____was my first love. (그녀는 나의 첫사랑이었다.)

10._____is doing his homework now. (그는 지금 그의 숙제를 하고 있다.)

---- **Exercise 1-1** --

다음 해석에 맞게 빈칸을 채우세요.

1.＿＿＿＿＿is mine. (그것은 나의 것이다.)

2.＿＿＿＿＿are on the basketball team. (너는 농구팀에 있다.)

3.＿＿＿＿＿looks beautiful. (그녀는 아름다워 보인다.)

4.＿＿＿＿＿is a nice car. (그것은 좋은 차다.)

5.＿＿＿＿＿is my mom. (그녀는 나의 엄마다.)

6.＿＿＿＿＿is very handsome. (그는 매우 잘 생겼다.)

7.＿＿＿＿＿know about me well. (그들은 나에 대해서 잘 안다.)

8.＿＿＿＿＿are rich. (그들은 부유하다.)

9.＿＿＿＿＿am your brother. (나는 너의 형이다.)

10.＿＿＿＿＿are twins. (우리는 쌍둥이다.)

---- **Exercise 2** --

다음 해석에 맞게 빈칸을 채우세요.

1. I like_____. (나는 너를 좋아한다.)

2. She doesn't love_____. (그녀는 그를 사랑하지 않는다.)

3. We have to finish_____as soon as possible.
(우리는 그것을 가능한 빨리 끝내야한다.)

4. Can you lend_____some money? (나 돈 좀 빌려줄 수 있니?)

5. I know_____very well. (나는 그들을 매우 잘 안다.)

6. They gave_____some money. (그들은 나에게 돈을 좀 줬다.)

7. He loves_____. (그는 너를 사랑한다.)

8. Don't send_____anything. (그녀에게 아무것도 보내지 마라.)

9. May I help_____? (제가 당신을 도와드릴까요?)

10. Is the book difficult for_____? (이 책은 우리에게 어렵나요?)

---- **Exercise 3** --

다음 해석에 맞게 빈칸을 채우세요.

1. This is_____car. (이것은 나의 차다.)

2. What is_____favorite color? (네가 가장 좋아하는 색깔은 무엇이니?)

3. She is_____wife. (그녀는 그의 아내다.)

4. Do you know_____names? (너는 그들의 이름들을 아니?)

5. What is_____hobby? (너의 취미는 뭐니?)

6. Where is_____bag? (나의 가방이 어디 있지?)

7. _____cat is under the table. (우리의 고양이는 탁자 아래에 있다.)

8. She is always on_____side. (그녀는 언제나 우리의 편이다.)

9. _____parties are always fun. (그들의 파티는 언제나 재미있다.)

10._____dream is to be a teacher. (나의 꿈은 선생님이 되는 것이다.)

---- **Exercise 3-1** ---

다음 해석에 맞게 빈칸을 채우세요.

1. Tom is _____ best friend. (Tom은 나의 가장 친한 친구이다.)

2. Give me _____ number right now. (지금 당장 그녀의 전화번호를 나에게 주시오.)

3. What is in _____ bag? (너의 가방 안에는 무엇이 있니?)

4. _____ team beat the other team again. (우리 팀이 또 상대팀을 이겼다.)

5. Jane is _____ girl friend. (Jane은 나의 여자 친구이다.)

6. Where is _____ dog? (우리의 개는 어디 있니?)

7. This is _____ first visit to Korea. (이번이 그의 첫 방한이다.)

8. Is this _____ number? (이게 그녀의 전화번호니?)

9. Can I use _____ phone? (내가 당신의 전화를 사용해도 될까요?)

10. _____ house is far from here. (그들의 집은 여기서 멀다.)

---- **Exercise 4** --

다음 해석에 맞게 빈칸을 채우세요.

1. _____ hate you. (나는 너를 싫어한다.)

2. He gave it to _____. (그는 그것을 나에게 줬다.)

3. I want to meet _____ wife. (나는 그의 아내를 만나기를 원한다.)

4. _____ stayed with me. (그들은 나와 머물렀다.)

5. Let me show _____ something. (내가 너에게 뭔가를 보여줄게.)

6. We respect _____ so much. (우리는 그를 매우 존경한다.)

7. _____ played soccer. (그는 축구를 했다.)

8. _____ friend played soccer. (그녀의 친구는 축구를 했다.)

9. She gave _____ new shoes. (그녀는 우리에게 새 신발을 줬다.)

10. I have a good relationship with _____. (나는 그들과 원만한 관계를 갖고 있다.)

---- **Exercise 5** --

다음 문장의 밑줄 친 부분을 바르게 고쳐 쓰세요.

1. This book is <u>me</u>. (이 책은 나의 것이다.)

2. Those books are <u>us</u>. (저 책들은 우리의 것이다.)

3. The ball is <u>her</u>. (그 공은 그녀의 것이다.)

4. That picture is <u>him</u>. (저 그림은 그의 것이다.)

5. These pens are <u>they</u>. (이 펜들은 그들의 것이다.)

6. This watch is <u>I</u>. (이 시계는 내 것이다.)

7. The cell phone is not <u>your</u>. (그 휴대폰은 너의 것이 아니다.)

8. The house is <u>we.</u> (그 집은 우리의 것이다.)

9. The purse is <u>her</u>. (그 지갑은 그녀의 것이다.)

10. This card is not <u>me.</u> (이 카드는 나의 것이 아니다.)

---- **Exercise 5-1** --

다음 문장의 밑줄 친 부분을 바르게 고쳐 쓰세요.

1. The car is <u>your</u>. (그 차는 당신의 것이다.)

2. The shirts are <u>us</u>. (그 셔츠들은 우리의 것이다.)

3. These earrings are <u>she</u>. (이 귀걸이들은 그녀의 것이다.)

4. This laptop is <u>your</u>. (이 노트북은 너의 것이다.)

5. This chair is <u>them</u>. (이 의자는 그들의 것이다.)

6. The money in your pocket is <u>me</u>. (네 주머니에 있는 돈은 내 것이다.)

7. This pair of shoes is <u>him</u>. (이 신발은 그의 것이다.)

8. The yellow cap is <u>her</u>. (그 노란 모자는 그녀의 것이다.)

9. This book is <u>us</u>. (이 책은 우리의 것이다.)

10. What is <u>I</u>? (나의 것은 무엇이니?)

Unit 3 명령문

- 긍정 명령문
- 부정 명령문

Gorilla Grammar

unit 3 명령문

1 긍정 명령문

: 주어를 생략하고 동사원형으로 시작. '~해라'로 해석

a. Be patient.

인내해라.

b. Study hard.

열심히 공부해라.

c. Keep calm.

침착해라.

2 부정 명령문

• Don't나 Never 뒤에 바로 동사원형을 두고 시작. '~하지 마라'로 해석

a. Don't be late.

늦지 마라.

b. Never cry.

결코 울지 마라.

c. Don't close the door.

그 문을 닫지 마라.

---- **Exercise 1** --

다음 문장을 명령문으로 바꾸세요.

1. You are kind to everyone.

→

2. You don't open the door.

→

3. You close the window.

→

4. You come here.

→

5. You are quiet.

→

---- **Exercise 1-1** --

다음 문장을 명령문으로 바꾸세요.

1. You do your homework right now.

→

2. You never tell a lie.

→

3. You are generous with your time.

→

4. You don't say that again.

→

5. You are not lazy.

→

---- **Exercise 2** ---

다음 문장을 영작하세요.

1. 안녕(goodbye)이라고 말하지 마.

→

2. 행복해라.

→

3. 다시는 나에게 전화하지 마.

→

4. 이리와.

→

5. 푹 자라. (soundly)

→

---- **Exercise 2-1** ---

다음 문장을 영작하세요.

1. 걱정하지 마.

→

2. 헬멧 없이 자전거 타지 마. (without a helmet)

→

3. 나를 봐라.

→

4. 지금 당장 너의 방을 청소해라. (right now)

→

5. 화내지 마라. (angry)

→

1 다음 밑줄 친 단어의 종류가 올바르게 짝지어진 것을 고르세요.

① He is in front of the <u>mirror</u>. (부사)
② She is <u>very</u> smart. (형용사)
③ They are <u>students</u>. (명사)
④ I am <u>his</u> best friend. (동사)
⑤ She <u>runs</u> fast. (부사)

2 다음 밑줄 친 부분 중 어법상 **틀린** 것을 고르세요.

① <u>He</u> is sleepy.
② <u>Her</u> friend is from America.
③ <u>Them</u> are nurses.
④ <u>My</u> sister is smart.
⑤ They met <u>him.</u>

3 두 단어의 관계가 나머지와 <u>다른</u> 하나는?

① he - him
② she - her
③ they - them
④ it - it
⑤ you - your

4 다음 주어진 단어들 중에서 명사를 꾸며주는 역할을 하는 것은?

① meet
② together
③ soft
④ price
⑤ run

5 다음 중 어법상 <u>어색한</u> 문장은?

① I always play with their.
② She met him yesterday.
③ They hurt him.
④ You sent me a book.
⑤ We discussed the topic with her.

6 다음 빈칸에 알맞지 <u>않은</u> 것은?

Kelly, don't_____ in the morning.

① run
② late
③ watch TV
④ drink too much
⑤ eat

7 다음 중 어법상 **틀린** 것은?

① They meet him.
② She told my a secret.
③ We made her a candle.
④ I like them very much.
⑤ He disappeared with his cat.

8 다음 빈칸에 알맞은 말이 순서대로 짝지어진 것은?

_____nickname is an angel because_____
is kind. Yesterday, I met_____and he
helped_____a lot.
(그의 별명은 천사야 왜냐하면 그가 친절하기 때
문이지. 어제, 나는 그를 만났고 그는 나를 많이
도와줬어.)

① He – he – his – me
② He – his – his – I
③ His – he – him – me
④ His – his – him – I
⑤ Him – he – his – me

9 다음 빈칸에 알맞은 말을 쓰세요.

My son is smart. _____ is a high school
student.

[**10~11**] 다음 대화의 빈칸에 알맞은 말을 고르세요.

10

A: Is this his book?
B: Yes, it's_____

① mine
② him
③ his
④ hers
⑤ ours

11

A: Sophie, this is Mr.Lee. I'm_____student.
B: Nice to meet you, Mr.Lee.

① her
② my
③ she
④ his
⑤ him

12 다음 빈칸에 적절한 표현을 **모두** 고르면?

He is_____teacher.

① my
② him
③ us
④ her
⑤ you

13 다음 빈칸에 들어갈 수 <u>없는</u> 말은?

> She met_____.

① you
② her
③ his
④ them
⑤ us

14 다음 빈칸에 알맞은 말을 쓰세요.

> Running in the hall is dangerous because
> the hall is very narrow. Please_____run
> here.

15 다음 중 어법상 <u>어색한</u> 것은?

① Be quiet.
② Not move again.
③ Help yourself.
④ Turn right at the corner.
⑤ Don't be rude.

16 다음 문장에서 <u>어색한</u> 부분을 찾아 어법에 맞게
고쳐 쓰세요.

> It's too cold. Please closes the window.

17 다음 문장의 밑줄 친 부분과 바꿔 쓸 수 있는
대명사는?

> <u>Jeremy and Mike</u> are good coworkers.

정답:_____

18 다음 빈칸에 공동으로 들어갈 인칭대명사를 써
넣으세요.

(1)_____sister is also a teacher.
(2) Nick gave_____a book.
(3)I met_____ yesterday.

[19-20] 다음 대화를 읽고, 물음에 답하세요.

> A: I met Linda yesterday. Do you know ⓐ___
> ?
> B: Sure, I also know ⓐ_____sister.
> A: Really? ⓑ_____are so pretty.
> B: Yes, I think so.

19
(1) ⓐ에 공통으로 들어갈 단어를 쓰세요.

정답:

(2) ⓑ에 들어갈 단어를 쓰세요.

정답:

20 윗글에서 부사가 몇 개 등장하는지 쓰세요.

정답: _____

Unit 4 be동사

- 동사의 종류
- be동사의 현재 및 과거형과 축약형
- be동사의 부정문
- be동사의 의문문

Gorilla Grammar

unit 4 be동사

1 동사의 종류

동사	be 동사	주어의 인칭에 따라 현재일 땐 (am, are, is), 과거일 땐 (was, were)
	일반동사	be 동사를 제외한 모든 동사

2 be동사의 현재 및 과거형과 축약형

		현재	과거
단수	1인칭	I am (I'm)	I was
	2인칭	you are (you're)	you were
	3인칭	he is (he's)	he was
		she is (she's)	she was
		it is (it's)	it was
복수	1인칭	we are (we're)	we were
	2인칭	you are (you're)	you were
	3인칭	they are (they're)	they were

a. She's pretty.

그녀는 예쁘다.

b. They're at the party.

그들은 파티에 있다.

c. I'm a student.

나는 학생이다.

d. We're friends.

우리는 친구이다.

e. It's nice.

그것은 멋지다.

EXERCISE 1

다음 문장의 빈칸에 am, are, is 중 알맞은 것을 쓰세요.

1. My sisters_____singers.

2. My father_____a dentist.

3. I_____your friend.

4. You_____the man.

5. He and I_____ten years old.

6. They_____very kind.

7. Where_____you from?

8. _____I doing well?

9. Mr. Kim_____good at swimming.

10. Her dad_____not generous.

---- **Exercise 1-1** --

다음 문장의 빈칸에 am, are, is 중 알맞은 것을 쓰세요.

1. He_____my best friend.

2. Tom Cruise_____a famous actor.

3. This watch_____not mine.

4. The books_____on the table.

5. The laptop_____very nice.

6. They_____so healthy.

7. I_____your father.

8. Which_____her favorite bag?

9. How_____you?

10. He_____gorgeous.

---- **Exercise 2** ---

다음 문장의 빈칸에 was, were 중 알맞은 것을 쓰세요.

1. Mr. Kim_____a police man.

2. You_____a student.

3. I_____so happy yesterday.

4. What_____her number?

5. He_____not like this.

6. They_____good at sport.

7. The refrigerator_____full.

8. We_____good friends.

9. Mr. Lee_____such a gentleman.

10. She_____my first love.

---- **Exercise 2-1** ---

다음 문장의 빈칸에 was, were 중 알맞은 것을 쓰세요.

1. You_____so beautiful.

2. She_____a doctor.

3. Her hobby_____table tennis.

4. He_____happy.

5. We_____high school students at that time.

6. They_____very rich 5 years ago.

7. Tom and Jane_____married to each other.

8. I_____a homeless child when I was young.

9. Where_____they last weekend?

10. What_____her opinion?

---- **Exercise 3** --

다음 문장의 밑줄 친 부분을 줄여서 다시 쓰세요.

1. <u>You are</u> 6 years old.

→

2. <u>He is</u> happy.

→

3. <u>They are</u> so kind.

→

4. <u>I am</u> your friend.

→

5. <u>She is</u> a doctor.

→

6. <u>We are</u> in your house.

→

7. <u>It is</u> sunny.

→

8. <u>That is</u> not your fault.

→

---- **Exercise 3-1** --

다음 문장의 밑줄 친 부분을 줄여서 다시 쓰세요.

1. <u>It is</u> time to leave.

→

2. <u>That is</u> a good idea.

→

3. <u>I am</u> a middle school student.

→

4. <u>He is</u> such a gentleman.

→

5. <u>She is</u> so lovely.

→

6. <u>We are</u> good at English.

→

7. <u>You are</u> gorgeous.

→

8. <u>They are</u> not idiots.

→

unit 4 be동사

  be동사의 부정문

• be동사 뒤에 not이나 never를 붙여주기만 하면 된다.

현재형의 부정문		
기본형	축약형 1	축약형 2
I am not a teacher.	I'm not a teacher.	없음
He is not a boy.	He's not a boy.	He isn't a boy.
She is not a girl.	She's not a girl.	She isn't a girl.
You are not a student.	You're not a student.	You aren't a student.
We are not friends.	We're not friends.	We aren't friends.
They are not friends.	They're not friends.	They aren't friends.

과거형의 부정문	
기본형	축약형
I was not a teacher.	I wasn't a teacher.
He was not a boy.	He wasn't a boy.
She was not a girl.	She wasn't a girl.
You were not a student.	You weren't a student.
We were not friends.	We weren't friends.
They were not friends.	They weren't friends.

---- **Exercise 1** --

다음 문장의 밑줄 친 부분을 줄여서 다시 쓰세요.

1. <u>He is</u> not my uncle.

2. She <u>is not</u> my daughter.

3. <u>They are</u> not my friends.

4. <u>We are</u> not students.

5. You <u>are not</u> bad.

6. <u>I am</u> not that kind of a man.

7. <u>We are</u> not happy.

8. You <u>are not</u> fat.

9. These <u>are not</u> mine.

10. <u>She is</u> not my girl friend.

EXERCISE 4

다음 문장의 밑줄 친 부분을 줄여서 다시 쓰세요.

1. She <u>is not</u> my cousin.

2. <u>He is</u> not my son.

3. <u>They are</u> not students.

4. This <u>is not</u> your money.

5. <u>She is</u> not a girl any more.

6. <u>He is</u> not gentle.

7. We <u>are not</u> sad.

8. <u>I am</u> not crazy.

9. <u>He is</u> not rich.

10. You <u>are not</u> hungry.

---- **Exercise 2** --

다음 문장을 부정문으로 바꾸어 쓰세요.

1. The boy was very friendly.

→

2. We are happy.

→

3. I am a boy.

→

4. She is so kind.

→

5. He was rich.

→

6. This book is mine.

→

7. Those were enough for me.

→

8. The chair is comfortable.

→

9. I was a painter.

→

10. They are from Korea.

→

---- **Exercise 2-1** --

다음 문장을 부정문으로 바꾸어 쓰세요.

1. We are good friends.

→

2. They were from Japan.

→

3. He is a famous singer.

→

4. You are tall.

→

5. He was handsome.

→

6. She is having dinner now.

→

7. We were going to go to school.

→

8. They are so friendly.

→

9. I was fine.

→

10. That is enough.

→

unit 4   be동사

 be동사의 의문문

- be동사를 문장 맨 앞으로 빼주고 뒤에 물음표를 붙여준다.

- 현재형

평서문	의문문
I am a teacher. / I'm a teacher	Am I a teacher?
He is a boy. / He's a boy.	Is he a boy?
She is a girl. / She's a girl.	Is she a girl?
You are a student. / You're a student.	Are you a student?
We are friends. / We're friends.	Are we friends?
They are friends. / They're friends.	Are they friends?

- 과거형

평서문	의문문
I was a teacher.	Was I a teacher?
He was a boy.	Was he a boy?
She was a girl.	Was she a girl?
You were a student.	Were you a student?
We were friends.	Were we friends?
They were friends.	Were they friends?

---- **Exercise 1** --

다음 문장을 의문문으로 바꾸어 쓰세요.

1. I was a student.

→

2. Tom is generous.

→

3. She was cute.

→

4. You were my friend.

→

5. She is beautiful.

→

6. Her name is Jane.

→

7. Red was my favorite color.

→

8. You are happy.

→

9. You were leaving.

→

10. They are good at swimming.

→

---- **Exercise 1-1** --

다음 문장을 의문문으로 바꾸어 쓰세요.

1. John was your roommate.

→

2. She is lovely.

→

3. He was from Brazil.

→

4. Tom is hungry.

→

5. You were alone.

→

6. I am single.

→

7. We are in the pool.

→

8. They were so kind.

→

9. She is smart.

→

10. He was good at running.

→

---- **Exercise 2** --

주어진 단어를 이용하여 영작하세요.

1. 그녀는 예쁘지 않다. (pretty)

→

2. 그는 매우 잘 생겼다. (handsome)

→

3. 그들은 친절하다. (kind)

→

4. 너는 혼자니? (alone)

→

5. 나는 집에 있다. (home)

→

6. 그녀는 아팠다. (sick)

→

7. 그는 일본인이 아니다. (Japanese)

→

8. 너는 지금 바쁘니? (busy)

→

9. 그것은 매우 아름다웠다. (beautiful)

→

10. 시간은 금이다. (gold)

→

---- **Exercise 2-1** --

주어진 단어를 이용하여 영작하세요.

1. 그녀는 지적이니? (intelligent)

→

2. Tom은 성실하니? (diligent)

→

3. 그녀는 키가 크지 않다. (tall)

→

4. 이 아기는 너무 귀엽다. (cute)

→

5. 그녀는 나의 첫사랑이었다. (first love)

→

6. 이 시계는 너의 것이니? (watch)

→

7. 그는 작년에 학생이었다. (last year)

→

8. 그들은 매우 키가 크다. (tall)

→

9. 그 영화는 매우 재미있었다. (fun)

→

10. 너와 나는 동갑이다. (the same age)

→

---- **Exercise 3** ---

다음 질문에 긍정과 부정으로 대답하세요.

1. Is she a nurse?

긍정 →

부정 →

2. Are you tired?

긍정 →

부정 →

3. Are you happy?

긍정 →

부정 →

4. Are they sad?

긍정 →

부정 →

5. Is he a gentleman?

긍정 →

부정 →

6. Was he smart at that time?

긍정 →

부정 →

7. Were they in the house?

긍정 →

부정 →

8. Was there a school?

긍정 →

부정 →

9. Was he an English teacher?

긍정 →

부정 →

10. Was it rainy yesterday?

긍정 →

부정 →

EXERCISE 3

다음 질문에 긍정과 부정으로 대답하세요.

1. Is the baby cute?

긍정 →

부정 →

2. Are we ready to go?

긍정 →

부정 →

3. Are you ok?

긍정 →

부정 →

4. Is Mrs. Lee a pilot?

긍정 →

부정 →

5. Are they your cousins?

긍정 →

부정 →

6. Was Mr. Kim upset?

긍정 →

부정 →

7. Was she supportive?

긍정 →

부정 →

8. Were you a doctor?

긍정 →

부정 →

9. Was he busy at that time?

긍정 →

부정 →

10. Were they good friends?

긍정 →

부정 →

Unit 5   일반 동사

- 일반동사의 3인칭 단수 현재형 만들기
- 일반동사의 과거형 만들기(규칙)
- 일반동사의 과거형 만들기(불규칙)
- 일반동사의 의문문 만들기
- 일반동사의 부정문 만들기

Gorilla Grammar

unit 5 일반 동사

 일반동사의 3인칭 단수 현재형 만들기

종류	방법	예시
대부분의 동사	동사원형에 -s를 붙인다.	begins, gives, rings, takes, likes …
-s, -ss, -x, -sh, -ch로 끝나는 동사	동사원형에 -es를 붙인다.	passes, finishes, watches …
자음+o 로 끝나는 동사	동사원형에 -es를 붙인다.	does, goes
자음+y 로 끝나는 동사	y를 i로 바꾸고, -es를 붙인다.	try → tries, study → studies
모음+y 로 끝나는 동사	그대로 -s를 붙인다.	enjoys, says, stays …

★ have의 3인칭 단수형: has

---- **Exercise 1** --

다음 밑줄 친 부분을 옳게 고치세요. (단, 현재시제를 사용하세요.)

1. He <u>eat</u> bread for lunch.

→

2. She <u>want</u> to go out.

→

3. He <u>go</u> to bed early.

→

4. We <u>has</u> a lot of books.

→

5. He <u>work</u> hard.

→

6. Tom <u>teach</u> them English.

→

7. She always <u>sleep</u> well.

→

8. He <u>enjoy</u> reading.

→

9. Time <u>fly</u>!

→

10. Jane <u>solve</u> problems.

→

---- Exercise 1-1 --

다음 밑줄 친 부분을 옳게 고치세요. (단, 현재시제를 사용하세요.)

1. Jane always <u>help</u> people in need.

→

2. I <u>watches</u> TV.

→

3. It <u>sound</u> great!

→

4. They <u>goes</u> to the movies.

→

5. He sometimes <u>lend</u> me money.

→

6. He <u>fix</u> it by himself.

→

7. She always <u>wait</u> for them.

→

8. That picture <u>look</u> great!

→

9. She <u>meet</u> Korean friends regularly.

→

10. He <u>hope</u> that he can solve the problem.

→

unit 5 일반 동사

 일반동사의 과거형 만들기 (규칙)

동사의 종류	만드는 방법	예시
대부분의 동사, -e로 끝나는 동사	동사원형 + (e)d를 붙인다.	worked, finished, helped,.. liked, danced …
자음+y 로 끝나는 동사	y를 i로 바꾸고, -ed를 붙인다.	try → tried, study → studied
모음+y 로 끝나는 동사	그대로 -ed를 붙인다.	enjoyed, stayed …
단모음+단자음 으로 끝나는 1음절 동사	자음을 한 번 더 쓰고 -ed를 붙인다.	stopped, planned …

---- **Exercise 1** --

다음 주어진 단어들의 과거형을 쓰세요.

1. rob _____   8. hate _____
2. agree _____   9. drop _____
3. marry _____   10. admit _____
4. hope _____   11. occur _____
5. love _____   12. fry _____
6. change _____   13. play _____
7. study _____   14. turn _____

---- **Exercise 1-1** --

다음 주어진 단어들의 과거형을 쓰세요.

1. stop _____   8. plan _____
2. climb _____   9. hurry _____
3. beg _____   10. offer _____
4. talk _____   11. call _____
5. close _____   12. die _____
6. carry _____   13. enjoy _____
7. clean _____   14. end _____

---- **Exercise 2** ---

다음 문장을 과거형 문장으로 변환하세요.

1. Traffic accidents occur very often.

→

2. I talk to you.

→

3. They call me John.

→

4. We play soccer together.

→

5. The store opens at 7a.m.

→

---- **Exercise 3** ---

다음 문장을 영작하세요. (규칙동사)

1. 그는 거기에 아주 오래 머물렀다. (stay, quite a long time)

→

2. 그들은 어제 컴퓨터 게임을 했다. (play)

→

3. 나는 친구들과 함께 서울에 방문했다. (visit)

→

4. Tom은 3년 전에 죽었다. (die)

→

5. 나는 오늘 아침에 영어공부를 열심히 했다. (study)

→

---- **Exercise 3-1** ---

다음 문장을 영작하세요. (규칙동사)

1. 그녀는 그 책들을 가방에 넣고 갔다. (carry, in the bag)

→

2. 그는 나의 집에 또 들어왔다. (enter)

→

3. 나는 그녀와 2일 전에 결혼했다. (marry)

→

4. 그는 선풍기로 그의 머리카락을 말렸다. (dry, a fan)

→

5. 그녀는 어제 이메일 주소를 변경했다. (address, yesterday)

→

unit 5 일반 동사

일반동사의 과거형 만들기 (불규칙)

기본형	과거형	의미	기본형	과거형	의미
be	was /were	이다, 있다	keep	kept	유지하다
become	became	되다	hurt	hurt	상처 내다
begin	began	시작하다	know	knew	알다
bring	brought	가져오다	leave	left	떠나다
build	built	짓다	lose	lost	잃다
buy	bought	사다	make	made	만들다
come	came	오다	meet	met	만나다
choose	chose	선택하다	put	put	놓다
cut	cut	자르다	read	read	읽다
do	did	하다	run	ran	뛰다
drink	drank	마시다	say	said	말하다
drive	drove	운전하다	see	saw	보다
eat	ate	먹다	sell	sold	팔다
feel	felt	느끼다	send	sent	보내다
find	found	발견하다	sing	sang	노래하다
get	got	얻다	sleep	slept	자다
give	gave	주다	take	took	취하다
go	went	가다	teach	taught	가르치다
grow	grew	자라다	tell	told	말하다
have	had	가지다	think	thought	생각하다
hear	heard	듣다	understand	understood	이해하다
hide	hid	숨기다	win	won	이기다
hit	hit	치다			

---- **Exercise 1** --

다음 주어진 단어들의 과거형을 쓰세요.

1. be	_____	8. get	_____
2. find	_____	9. do	_____
3. come	_____	10. build	_____
4. give	_____	11. go	_____
5. grow	_____	12. buy	_____
6. become	_____	13. hurt	_____
7. hear	_____	14. feel	_____

---- **Exercise 1-1** --

다음 주어진 단어들의 과거형을 쓰세요.

1. make	_____	8. read	_____
2. send	_____	9. teach	_____
3. meet	_____	10. say	_____
4. tell	_____	11. take	_____
5. put	_____	12. sell	_____
6. know	_____	13. see	_____
7. run	_____	14. think	_____

---- **Exercise 2** --

다음 문장을 과거형 문장으로 변환하세요.

1. I make myself understood.

→

2. She sleeps less than 5 hours.

→

3. I teach her how to cook.

→

4. They give me a bouquet of flowers.

→

5. They keep the secret.

→

6. The wind begins to blow.

→

7. I hide the comic book under the bed.

→

8. My brother drives the bus.

→

9. We sing a song together.

→

10. I drink alcohol almost everyday.

→

---- **Exercise 2-1** --

다음 문장을 과거형 문장으로 변환하세요.

1. I want to play basketball.

→

2. She moves toward the window.

→

3. We win the game without your help.

→

4. I see her in the hospital.

→

5. He feels nervous before a test.

→

6. I'll stay at home on Sunday.

→

7. She enters the room.

→

8. I will pass the exam.

→

9. I am not a stranger.

→

10. She calls me several times.

→

---- **Exercise 3** ---

다음 주어진 단어를 적절히 변형하여 영작하세요.

1. Tom은 그녀를 병원에 데려갔다. (bring)

→

2. 그녀는 어제 나를 때렸다. (hit)

→

3. 그녀는 나에게 사탕을 주었다. (give)

→

4. Jane은 안녕이란 말도 안하고 떠났다. (leave, without, saying)

→

5. 나는 그에게 뭔가 잘못된 것을 말했다. (tell, something wrong)

→

6. Mr. Lee는 지난 일요일에 책을 읽었다. (read)

→

7. 그는 칼로 종이를 잘랐다. (cut, a knife)

→

8. 나는 어제 영어 시험을 쳤다. (take)

→

9. 그들은 3년 전에 그 다리를 건설했다. (build)

→

10. 그는 그녀를 잘 알고 있었다. (know)

→

---- **Exercise 3-1** --

다음 주어진 단어를 적절히 변형하여 영작하세요.

1. 그는 나에 관한 모든 것을 이해했다. (understand, everything about)

→

2. 사람들은 그들의 집들을 잃었다. (lose)

→

3. 나는 너의 모든 것을 좋아 했었다. (like)

→

4. 그녀는 그 책을 어제 읽었다. (read)

→

5. 우리는 점심으로 피자를 먹었다. (eat)

→

6. 나는 Sally 대신 Jane을 선택했다. (choose, instead of)

→

7. 나는 어제 자기 전에 샤워를 했다. (take, going)

→

8. 나는 그가 수다쟁이라고 생각했다. (think that, talkative)

→

9. 그는 그 시계를 찾았다. (find)

→

10. 수업이 10분 만에 끝났다. (end, in)

→

 일반동사의 의문문 만들기

평서문	의문문
I have a dog.	Do I have a dog?
He has a dog.	Does he have a dog?
She meets a boy.	Does she meet a boy?
You meet a girl.	Do you meet a girl?
We do our homework.	Do we do our homework?
They do their homework.	Do they do their homework?
She met a boy.	Did she meet a boy?
You met a girl.	Did you meet a girl?

★ 만드는 방법

가장 먼저 동사를 확인하여 일반 동사일 경우 do, does, did 중
적절한 것을 선택하여 문장 맨 앞으로 꺼내준다.

뒤에 나오는 동사가 원형을 유지하는지 꼭 확인한다.

★ do, does, did 선택 방법

- 확인한 일반 동사가 과거형일 때 → did
- 확인한 일반 동사가 3인칭 단수형일 때 → does
- 확인한 일반 동사가 그밖에 나머지 일 때 → do

- She <u>meets</u> a boy. (does를 선택)
- <u>Does</u> she <u>meet</u> a boy? (동사원형 꼭 확인)

★ 대답하기

질문에 사용된 do, does, did를 그대로 사용한다.

- Do you have a car? → Yes, I do. / No, I don't.
- Does she meet him? → Yes, she does. / No, she doesn't.
- Did she meet him? → Yes, she did. / No, she didn't.

---- **Exercise 1** ---

다음 현재시제로 쓴 문장을 의문문으로 변환하세요.

1. He dries his hair with this towel.

→

2. She runs fast.

→

3. They go to church every Sunday.

→

4. I need a doctor.

→

5. We want to solve the problem.

→

6. Tom eats a lot.

→

7. He gives me some money.

→

8. I know her well.

→

9. She enjoys watching the movie.

→

10. He misses her so much.

→

---- **Exercise 1-1** --

다음 과거시제로 쓴 문장을 의문문으로 변환하세요.

1. She went to the movies.

→

2. He slept well.

→

3. You opened the door.

→

4. They remembered you.

→

5. The plane arrived on time.

→

6. She loved me.

→

7. He enjoyed singing.

→

8. She watched the play.

→

9. They lent me the chair.

→

10. The lion pushed the bus.

→

---- **Exercise 1-2** --

다음 문장을 의문문으로 변환하세요.

1. He borrowed this car for a week.

→

2. She rides a horse.

→

3. Tom liked you.

→

4. I love you.

→

5. They go to church.

→

6. We made this cake for him.

→

7. She listens to music.

→

8. I bought a pair of shoes.

→

9. We need your help.

→

10. She leaves on time.

→

EXERCISE 1

다음 문장을 의문문으로 변환하세요.

1. He solves mysteries.

→

2. We ride bicycles together.

→

3. The gorilla learned to speak.

→

4. My dad gave me a present.

→

5. You finished your homework.

→

6. He met her last Sunday.

→

7. They helped me a lot.

→

8. We eat meat for dinner.

→

9. He comes home early.

→

10. They loved us.

→

---- **Exercise 2** --

다음 질문에 알맞은 대답을 쓰세요.

1. Do you want this pen?

긍정 →

부정 →

2. Did he say yes?

긍정 →

부정 →

3. Do you want something to drink?

긍정 →

부정 →

4. Did you solve it?

긍정 →

부정 →

5. Do I know you?

긍정 →

부정 →

---- **Exercise 2-1** --

다음 질문에 알맞은 대답을 쓰세요.

1. Did they pass the exam?

긍정 →

부정 →

2. Did the baby cry?

긍정 →

부정 →

3. Did she leave early?

긍정 →

부정 →

4. Do they know you?

긍정 →

부정 →

5. Does he play the piano?

긍정 →

부정 →

unit 5 일반 동사

 5 일반동사의 부정문 만들기

	평서문	부정문
현재	I have a dog.	I don't(do not) have a dog.
	He has a dog.	He doesn't(does not) have a dog.
	She meets a boy.	She doesn't(does not) meet a boy.
	You meet a girl.	You don't(do not) meet a girl.
	We do our homework.	We don't(do not) do our homework.
	They do their homework.	They don't(do not) do their homework.
과거	She met a boy.	She didn't(did not) meet a boy.
	They did their homework.	They didn't(did not) do their homework.

★ 만드는 방법

가장 먼저 동사를 확인하여 일반 동사일 경우

do, does, did 중 적절한 것 선택하여 뒤에 not을 붙여준다.

★ do, does, did 선택 방법

- 확인한 일반 동사가 과거형일 때 → did

- 확인한 일반 동사가 3인칭 단수형일 때 → does

- 확인한 일반 동사가 그 밖에 나머지 일 때 → do

- She meets a boy. (does를 선택)

- She doesn't meet a boy. (동사원형 꼭 확인)

---- **Exercise 1** --

다음 주어진 문장을 부정문으로 바꾸세요.

1. I miss her.

→

2. The store opens at 10 a.m.

→

3. They fought for liberty.

→

4. She talked to him.

→

5. She lives in Busan.

→

6. You bought the car.

→

7. She played the violin.

→

8. He drives a car.

→

9. They know each other.

→

10. I did it.

→

---- **Exercise 1-1** --

다음 주어진 문장을 부정문으로 바꾸세요.

1. I did something wrong.

→

2. She does something wrong.

→

3. They do something wrong.

→

4. She took a bus.

→

5. They have dinner.

→

6. We do it well.

→

7. I asked him a favor.

→

8. She often lends him some books.

→

9. We brought the umbrellas.

→

10. He sleeps deeply.

→

1 다음 중 밑줄 친 부분의 쓰임이 잘못된 것은?

① <u>Are</u> you a student?
② Kate <u>are</u> friendly.
③ We <u>are</u> friends.
④ <u>Is</u> he kind?
⑤ They <u>are</u> students.

2 다음 중 줄임말이 바르지 못한 것은?

① <u>She's</u> very upset.
② <u>This's</u> mine.
③ This <u>isn't</u> my book.
④ <u>We're</u> not busy.
⑤ You <u>aren't</u> lucky.

[**3-4**] 다음 문장을 우리말과 뜻이 같도록 바꿔 쓰세요.

3 We are late.

→ _____

(우리는 늦지 않는다.)

4 He was a painter.

→ _____

(그는 화가가 아니었다.)

5 다음 중 be 동사의 쓰임이 올바른 것을 고르세요.

① I are a singer.
② My uncle, Sam are an engineer.
③ Mary and Jennifer is in the library.
④ Justin is looking forward to going there.
⑤ His books is on the desk.

6 다음 빈칸에 들어갈 말로 알맞은 것은?

James and Julie_____my best friends.

① am
② are
③ is
④ do
⑤ does

[**7-8**] 다음 빈칸에 들어갈 수 없는 것을 고르세요.

7

Anne_____her MP3 player all the time.

① has
② carries
③ listening
④ takes
⑤ plays

8

> _____ is in front of the bank.

① Mr. Kim
② Sam
③ He and I
④ Your dad
⑤ My boss

9 문장을 주어진 주어로 바꾸어 다시 쓰세요.

(1) They walk to school.

→ He_____

(2) I watch basketball on TV every weekend.

→ She_____

(3) He always doesn't bring his textbooks.

→ I_____

(4) Tom has three dogs.

→ They_____

10 빈칸에 들어갈 수 없는 것은?

> Mr. John_____English.

① speak
② teaches
③ learns
④ studies
⑤ reads

11 의미가 통하도록 주어진 말을 바르게 배열하세요.

> in, the piano, she, the school band, plays

→ _____

12 다음 글의 밑줄 친 부분 중 어법상 어색한 것은?

> ①It's Saturday. He ②get up at ten. In the morning, He plays soccer with his friends. In the afternoon, he ③plays baseball with his brother. He ④is very tired on every Saturday, but it ⑤is his favorite day of the week.

[13-14] 다음 대화의 빈칸에 들어갈 알맞은 응답을 고르세요.

13

> A : Is the game exciting?
> B : _____ It is very boring.

① Yes, it is.　　　② No, it isn't.
③ Yes, I do.　　　④ No, I don't.
⑤ Sure, I do.

14

> A : Are you coming from Vietnam?
> B : _____ I am coming from Korea.

① Yes, I am.　　　② No, I am not.
③ Yes, I do.　　　④ No, I don't.
⑤ Sure, I do.

15 다음 문장에서 어법상 어색한 부분을 찾으세요.

> ①Does ②your dad ③gives ④you a ride ⑤for you?

16 다음 문장을 의문문으로 바르게 전환한 것은?

> Maggie knows the story.

① Do Maggie know the story?
② Do Maggie knows the story?
③ Does Maggie know the story?
④ Does Maggie knows the story?
⑤ Does Maggie is know the story?

[17-18] 다음 중 어법상 어색한 것을 고르세요.

17

① Jill doesn't have money.
② She and I don't know the answer.
③ Does your dad always busy?
④ Do you visit your grandparents regularly?
⑤ I don't watch TV at all.

18

① She doesn't always has breakfast.
② Does he play soccer well?
③ Is your mom worried about you?
④ Do you understand me?
⑤ Jack and Jill aren't very happy with their score.

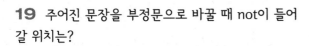

19 주어진 문장을 부정문으로 바꿀 때 not이 들어 갈 위치는?

① You ② were ③ in ④ the ⑤ library yesterday.

20 다음 대화의 빈칸에 알맞은 말을 쓰세요.

A : _____you at home yesterday?
B : No, I_____in the library.

Unit 6   현재진행형

- 동사의 ing형 만들기
- 현재진행형의 의문문과 부정문 및 대답하기
- 현재와 현재진행형의 비교

Gorilla Grammar

unit 6 현재진행형

• 현재진행형의 기본형은 am/are/is +ing 이며, 지금 현재 진행되고 있는 일을 나타내고자 할 때 쓴다.

 동사의 ing형 만들기

대부분의 동사	-ing	go - going do - doing sell - selling study - studying
자음 + -e 로 끝나는 동사	e를 빼고 -ing	make - making give - giving
-ie 로 끝나는 동사	ie를 y로 바꾸고 -ing	lie - lying die - dying
단모음 + 단자음 으로 끝나는 동사	마지막 자음을 한 번 더 쓰고 -ing	hit - hitting cut - cutting run - running stop - stopping

• The students are playing soccer now.

  그 학생들은 지금 축구를 하고 있는 중이다.

• I am studying English now.

  나는 지금 영어를 공부하고 있는 중이다.

• She is running toward the building now.

  그녀는 지금 빌딩을 향해 달려가고 있는 중이다.

---- **Exercise 1** --

다음 주어진 동사들의 +ing을 쓰세요.

1. read	_____	8. teach	_____
2. hit	_____	9. go	_____
3. lie	_____	10. have	_____
4. do	_____	11. buy	_____
5. stop	_____	12. say	_____
6. study	_____	13. make	_____
7. admit	_____	14. feel	_____

---- **Exercise 1-1** --

다음 주어진 동사들의 +ing을 쓰세요.

1. sell	_____	8. see	_____
2. lie	_____	9. know	_____
3. run	_____	10. say	_____
4. find	_____	11. grow	_____
5. die	_____	12. be	_____
6. cut	_____	13. build	_____
7. take	_____	14. do	_____

---- **Exercise 2** --

다음 주어진 문장을 현재진행형 문장으로 바꿔 쓰세요.

1. Mom washes the dishes.

→

2. I sleep in the room.

→

3. He plays the computer game.

→

4. Jane has dinner.

→

5. He comes home late.

→

6. Dad walks fast.

→

7. I take the bus.

→

8. They ride horses.

→

9. She plays the guitar.

→

10. You wear a pretty dress.

→

EXERCISE 2

다음 주어진 문장을 현재진행형 문장으로 바꿔 쓰세요.

1. I catch the ball.

→

2. They eat pizza.

→

3. I use this pen.

→

4. We open the door.

→

5. You study hard.

→

6. He runs away from them.

→

7. We cry loudly.

→

8. She takes a picture.

→

9. He passes the line.

→

10. The horse runs fast.

→

2 현재진행형의 의문문과 부정문 및 대답하기

---- **Exercise 1** --

다음 문장을 의문문과 부정문으로 바꾸세요.

1. She is watching the accident.

→

→

2. I am eating chicken now.

→

→

3. He is doing his homework.

→

→

4. She is wearing new shoes.

→

→

5. They are writing a letter.

→

→

6. I am having lunch now.

→

→

7. He is cleaning the windows.

→

→

8. We are playing the piano.

→

→

9. She is singing a song.

→

→

10. He is drawing a picture.

→

→

---- **Exercise 1-1** --

다음 문장을 의문문과 부정문으로 바꾸세요.

1. I am reading a book.

→

→

2. The girl is driving a car.

→

→

3. They are fishing illegally.

→

→

4. We are going to the gym.

→

→

5. He is running toward her.

→

→

6. She is sleeping.

→

→

7. They are shouting loudly.

→

→

8. The bird is flying high.

→

→

9. We are lifting stones.

→

→

10. I'm putting the presents into the box.

→

→

---- **Exercise 2** --

다음 문장에 긍정과 부정으로 대답하세요.

1. Are you reading a novel?

긍정 →

부정 →

2. Are you running fast?

긍정 →

부정 →

3. Is your mom cooking now?

긍정 →

부정 →

4. Is he studying Japanese?

긍정 →

부정 →

5. Are we going to the department store?

긍정 →

부정 →

6. Are they watching TV?

긍정 →

부정 →

----

7. Is he serving in the army?

긍정 →

부정 →

8. Is my brother moving to Seoul?

긍정 →

부정 →

9. Is she playing soccer?

긍정 →

부정 →

10. Are you going to school?

긍정 →

부정 →

unit 6   현재진행형

3   현재와 현재진행형의 비교

- 현재: 현재의 사실, 상태, 습관, 반복적 행위를 나타낼 때
- 현재진행: 현재 행해지고 있는 동작의 연속을 나타낸다

a. He plays the piano. (every Sunday)

그는 피아노를 연주한다. (매주 일요일마다)

b. He is playing the piano (now).

그는 지금 피아노를 연주하고 있는 중이다.

- -

★ a.는 지금 당장 피아노를 연주하고 있는 것이 아니라 He에 대한 일종의 배경 설명이 된다.

즉, 그는 매주 일요일마다 피아노를 치는 사람이라는 것이다.

반면에 b.는 지금 당장 피아노를 치는 일에 주력하고 있다는 것을 암시한다.

a. He is honest. (usually)

그는 정직하다.

b. He is being honest. (temporarily)

그는 <u>정직해하고 있다.</u>

- -

★ a.에서 그는 보통 정직한 사람이라는 뜻이고, b.에서 그는 평소에는 아닐지라도

지금 순간은 <u>정직해하고 있는</u> 집중도를 나타낸다.

---- **Exercise 1** ---

다음 중 올바른 표현을 고르세요.

1. They (play / are playing) soccer every Sunday.

2. My sister (watches / is watching) TV now.

3. We (jog / are jogging) now.

4. It (rains / is raining) a lot in summer.

5. Watch out! A rock (falls / is falling).

6. She (usually reads / is uaually reading) a novel in the restroom.

7. Every object (falls / is falling) at the same speed.

8. My brother (plays / is playing) basketball now.

9. This car (belongs / is belonging) to me.

10. 1 (know / am knowing) that the earth is round.

---- **Exercise 1-1** --

다음 중 올바른 표현을 고르세요.

1. We (hate / are hating) bugs.

2. Tom (takes / is taking) a shower at the moment.

3. The water (boils / is boiling). Let me turn it off now.

4. A : What (do you do / are you doing)?
   B : I am a dentist.

5. Usually, I (go / am going) to bed before midnight.

6. Water (boils / is boiling) at 100℃.

7. A : What are you doing now?
   B : I (listen / am listening) to the music.

8. She is not available now. She (talks / is talking) on the phone.

9. I (swim / am swimming) in the river now.

10. Excuse me, do you (speak / be speaking) English?

---- **Exercise 2** --

다음 주어진 문장을 현재진행형 문장으로 영작하세요.

1. 나는 피아노를 연주하고 있지 않다.

→

2. 그녀는 너를 기다리고 있는 중이다.

→

3. 나는 Tom과 전화로 이야기하는 중이다. (talk on)

→

4. 그들은 축구를 하고 있다.

→

5. 그녀는 수영을 하고 있지 않다.

→

6. 나는 빗속을 걷고 있다. (in the rain)

→

7. 너는 크게 말하고 있지 않다. (loudly)

→

8. 그녀는 그 아이에게 미소짓고 있다. (smile at)

→

9. Mr. Kim은 낚시를 하고 있다. (fish)

→

10. 그녀는 열심히 공부하고 있지 않다.

→

---- **Exercise 3** ---

다음 주어진 문장을 적절한 시제를 사용하여 영작하세요.

1. 물이 끓고 있다. (boil)

→

2. 나는 일요일마다 교회에 간다. (go to church)

→

3. 그녀는 사무실에서 일한다.(office)

→

4. 나는 자고 있지 않다. (sleep)

→

5. 나는 자정이 되기 전에 잔다. (go to bed)

→

6. 그녀는 저녁식사 중이 아니다. (have)

→

7. Tom은 강아지 3마리를 가지고 있다. (have)

→

8. 그녀는 갈색 눈동자를 갖고 있다. (have)

→

9. 그 가게는 오전 7시에 연다. (open)

→

10. 그 소년은 샤워중이 아니다. (take)

→

EXERCISE 3

다음 주어진 문장을 적절한 시제를 사용하여 영작하세요.

1. 그는 솔직하다. (honest)

→

2. 그녀는 그를 향해 지금 달려가고 있는 중이다.

→

3. 그녀는 그 가방을 가지고 있지 않다.

→

4. 그들은 농구를 하고 있는 중이다.

→

5. 나는 그에게 그 이야기를 하지 않았다.

→

6. 나는 일요일마다 영화를 본다.

→

7. 나는 영화를 보는 중이다.

→

8. 그는 어제 교회에 가지 않았다.

→

9. 토끼는 긴 귀를 가지고 있다.

→

10. 그 개는 지금 짖고 있다. (bark)

→

Unit 7 미래를 나타내는 will과 be going to

- will과 be going to의 비교
- 부정문과 의문문 만들기

Gorilla Grammar

unit 7 미래를 나타내는 will과 be going to

1 will과 be going to의 비교

	will + 동사원형	be going to + 동사원형
a. 미래 종류	의지 미래: ~할 것이다, ~하겠다.	예정 미래: ~할 예정이다
b. 대화 안에서	즉석에서 결정	이미 예정됨

a. 미래 종류

- I will help the girls someday.

  (의지 미래: 나는 그 소녀들을 언젠가 도울거야.)

- I am going to help the girls this summer.

  (예정 미래: 나는 이번 여름에 그 소녀들을 도울 예정이다.)

b. 대화 안에서

★ 즉석에서 결정

A: We are out of milk!

　우리 우유가 떨어졌어.

B: I will buy some milk.

　내가 좀 사올게.

★ 예정된 일

A: We are out of milk!

　우리 우유가 떨어졌어.

B: I know. I'm going to buy some milk.

　알고 있어. 사러갈 예정이야.

---- **Exercise 1** ---

다음 주어진 문장에서 <u>틀린</u> 부분을 찾아서 고치세요. (미래표현 유지)

1. He will goes to school soon.

2. She is going to meeting him.

3. He will passes the exam.

4. I am going call you.

5. We will being fine.

6. Are you go to take a bus?

7. They will cleaned the room.

8. She is going to telling you something.

9. I will graduating from middle school soon.

10. Will you to marry her?

---- **Exercise 2** --

다음 주어진 단어를 이용하여 영작하세요.

1. 나는 이번 여름에 일본에 갈 예정이다. (be going to)

→

2. 나는 내 방을 청소할 것이다. (will)

→

3. 나는 의사가 될 것이다. (will)

→

4. 아빠가 우리에게 점심을 만들어주실 예정이다. (be going to)

→

5. 나는 오늘밤 그녀에게 그 사건에 대해 말할 것이다. (will, accident)

→

---- **Exercise 2-1** --

다음 주어진 단어를 이용해서 영작하세요.

1. 그의 꿈은 언젠가 이루어질 것이다. (will)

→

2. 나는 내년에 그를 방문할 예정이다. (be going to)

→

3. 나는 내일 수영하러갈 예정이다. (be going to)

→

4. 언젠가, 그녀는 돌아올 것이다. (will)

→

5. 너무 많은 분노는 널 죽일 것이다. (anger, will)

→

unit 7 미래를 나타내는 will과 be going to

2 부정문과 의문문 만들기

기본형	will ('ll)	be going to
부정문	will not (won't)	be not going to
의문문	Will 주어 + 동사원형~?	be 주어 going to ~?

- She will be a doctor. (=She'll be a doctor.)

  그녀는 의사가 될 것이다.

- She will not be a doctor. (=She won't be a doctor.)

  그녀는 의사가 되지 않을 것이다.

- Will she be a doctor?

  그녀는 의사가 될까?

- We are going to go on a picnic.

  우리는 소풍갈 예정이다.

- We are not going to go on a picnic.

  우리는 소풍갈 예정이 아니다.

- Are you going to go on a picnic?

  너는 소풍갈 예정이니?

---- **Exercise 1** --

다음 주어진 문장을 의문문과 부정문으로 고치세요.

1. She will be ok.

의문문 →

부정문 →

2. He will come back.

의문문 →

부정문 →

3. She will drive me crazy.

의문문 →

부정문 →

4. I am going to see you soon.

의문문 →

부정문 →

5. We will visit America.

의문문 →

부정문 →

---- **Exercise 1-1** ---

다음 주어진 문장을 의문문과 부정문으로 고치세요.

1. It will rain tomorrow.

의문문 →

부정문 →

2. He will call us.

의문문 →

부정문 →

3. You are going to go home.

의문문 →

부정문 →

4. They are going to have dinner.

의문문 →

부정문 →

5. I will pass the exam.

의문문 →

부정문 →

---- **Exercise 2** ---

다음 주어진 문장을 영작하세요.

1. 창문 좀 닫아 줄래? (will)

→

2. 그것은 정말 지루할 것이다. (will)

→

3. 우리는 함께 춤을 추지 않을 것이다. (be going to)

→

4. 나는 오늘 늦게 잘 예정이다. (be going to)

→

5. 그는 선생님이 될 것인가? (will)

→

---- **Exercise 2-1** --

다음 주어진 문장을 영작하세요.

1. 이번 주 일요일에 교회에 갈 예정이니? (be going to)

→

2. 그는 그 음식을 주문할 예정이다. (be going to, order)

→

3. 나는 언젠가 미국에서 살 것이다. (will, someday)

→

4. 너는 그에게 초콜릿을 줄 예정이니? (be going to)

→

5. 그녀는 이번 여름에 강에서 수영을 하지 않을 것이다. (will)

→

1 다음 밑줄 친 부분 중 어법상 틀린 것은?

① He is <u>helping</u> his parents.
② The kid is <u>cutting</u> the cake.
③ Ann is <u>swimming</u> in the pool.
④ They are <u>learning</u> English now.
⑤ Are you <u>waitting</u> for someone?

2 주어진 우리말을 영어로 옮길 때 빈칸에 알맞은 말을 고르세요.

> 나는 James에게 이메일을 보내고 있다.
> =I _____ an e-mail to James.

① sent
② am send
③ sending
④ will send
⑤ am sending

3 다음 문장의 빈칸에 들어갈 동사 형태로 알맞지 않은 것을 고르세요.

> He is_____in his classroom.

① sing
② reading
③ talking
④ studying
⑤ sleeping

4 다음 문장을 부정문으로 바꿀 때 not이 들어갈 위치로 알맞은 곳은?

> I ①am ②looking ③for ④my mother's ⑤cell phone.

5 다음 문장을 현재진행형으로 바꿔 쓰세요.

> Do you read a newspaper?
>
> → _____

6 다음 밑줄 친 부분 중 어법상 틀린 것은?

Mom: ①<u>Are you doing</u> your homework, Tom?
Tom: ②<u>No, I'm reading</u> a comic book.
Mom: Well, ③<u>Will you help</u> me? ④<u>I need</u> some milk. Will you go to the market and buy some milk?
Tom: Sure, ⑤<u>I won't go</u>.

7 다음 빈칸에 들어갈 수 있는 것은?

> Jason is reading a book_____.

① now   ② tomorrow
③ this weekend   ④ yesterday
⑤ last Sunday

8 다음 중 문장의 밑줄 친 부분과 바꿔 쓸 수 있는 것은?

> They <u>are going to</u> visit their aunt.

① can   ② may
③ will   ④ must
⑤ have to

9 다음 중 어법상 어색한 것은?

① He will dance and sing tonight.
② Lions usually live together.
③ We didn't arrive at the village last night.
④ She is going to call me yesterday.
⑤ I will stay here for two more nights.

10 다음 문장을 의문문으로 바르게 전환한 것은?

> She will turn down the music.

① Will turn she down the music?
② Will she turn down the music?
③ She is going to turn down the music?
④ Will she turns down the music?
⑤ She will turn down the music?

11 다음 문장에서 어법상 어색한 부분을 고르세요.

> People ①will not ②breathes ③under the
> sea, ④because they need air ⑤to breathe.

[12-13] 빈칸에 들어갈 말로 알맞은 것을 고르세요.

12

> Bill will_____the baseball team.

① join   ② joins
③ joined   ④ joining
⑤ is joining

13

> She is going to_____to the concert.

① go   ② going
③ went   ④ gone
⑤ will go

14 주어진 문장과 의미가 비슷하도록 변형시킨 것은?

> I will never believe you again.

① I am never believe you again.
② I will believe you again.
③ I will never going to believe you again.
④ I am never going to believe you again.
⑤ I will going to never believe you again.

15 빈칸에 들어갈 수 없는 것은?

Some people will visit our house _____.

① tomorrow   ② this morning
③ last year   ④ next month
⑤ soon

16 괄호안의 동사를 알맞은 형태로 바꿔 쓰세요.

(1) Jack is going to go to bed soon, so
he is_____(take) a shower now.

(2) Amy will take an exam tomorrow, so
she is_____(study) hard now.

17 다음 밑줄 친 부분과 바꿔 쓸 수 있는 것은?

(1) Paul is going to arrive soon.
(2) Can you open the window for me?

① may
② must
③ will
④ should
⑤ could

18 다음 중 어법상 틀린 것은?

① Can you come to my house?
② We should do our homework.
③ Are she going to come here, too?
④ Should we borrow some book?
⑤ Will you go to the library with me?

19 다음 중 밑줄 친 부분이 어법상 틀린 것은?

A: ①Are you ②listening to music now?
B: ③No, ④I don't. I ⑤am reading a magazine.

20 주어진 단어를 사용하여 현재진행형 문장을 완성
하세요.

(1) Sorry, I am busy now. I_____ _____my
homework. (do)

(2)_____you_____at the moment?
(work)

(3) Jeremy_____ _____next to his mom.
(sit)

Unit 8   비인칭 주어 It

Gorilla Grammar

- 날씨, 계절, 날짜, 명암, 시간, 거리, 막연한 상황 등을 나타낼 때
  주어자리를 비워두지 않기 위해 사용한다.

  - It is raining now. (날씨)
    지금 비가 내리고 있다.

  - It is summer now. (계절)
    이제 여름이다.

  - It is bright in the living room. (명암)
    거실은 밝다.

  - It is three o'clock. (시간)
    세시다.

  - It's about 10 kilometers. (거리)
    대략 10킬로미터이다.

  - It's August 21st today. (날짜)
    오늘은 8월 21일이다.

  ★ 막연한 상황 예문
  - How's it going?

---- **Exercise 1** --

대명사 It을 써서 다음 문장을 영작하세요.

1. 오늘은 날씨가 화창하다. (fine)

→

2. 지금은 겨울이다.

→

3. 지금 몇 시야?

→

4. 11시 30분이야.

→

5. 오늘 무슨 요일이야? (what day)

→

6. 금요일이야.

→

7. 비가 오고 있다.

→

8. 어제는 추웠다.

→

9. 얼마나 머니? (far)

→

10. 5km정도 된다. (about)

→

---- **Exercise 1-1** --

대명사 It을 써서 다음 문장을 영작하세요.

1. 오늘은 수요일이다.

→

2. 지금은 오후 5시다.

→

3. 그것은 매우 쉽다.

→

4. 오늘은 매우 덥다.

→

5. 지금은 겨울이다.

→

6. 지금 몇시야?

→

7. 그것은 사실이다.

→

8. 그것은 나였다.

→

9. 어제는 매우 더웠다.

→

10. 지금 밖에 비가 오고 있다.

→

Unit 9   There is / There are

- There이 맨 앞에 나온 문장의 수일치

- 의문문과 부정문 만들기

Gorilla Grammar

1 There이 맨 앞에 나온 문장의 수일치

• There이 문장 맨 앞에 나오는 경우 there은 주어가 아니며, there 뒤에 도치가 일어난다. 따라서 동사 뒤에 나오는 명사(즉, 주어)에 수일치를 맞춰준다.

> • There is an apple on the table.
>   V   S
> 테이블 위에 사과 하나가 있다.

> • There are some apples on the table.
>   V   S
> 테이블 위에 사과들이 있다.

2 의문문과 부정문 만들기

• 특별한 것은 없고, be 동사의 부정문, 의문문 만드는 방법과 동일하다.

> • Is there a cup in the box?
>   컵 하나 있니?
> -Yes, there is. /No, there isn't.
>   응, 있어. /아니, 없어.
> • Are there cups in the box?
>   컵들이 있니?
> -Yes, there are. /No, there aren't.
>   응, 있어. / 아니, 없어.
> • There is not a book on the desk.
>   책상 위에 책 한 권이 없다.
> • There are not some books on the desk.
>   책상 위에 책들이 없다.

---- **Exercise 1** ---

다음 문장에서 문법적으로 틀린 부분을 찾아 고치세요.

1. There are a car.

→

2. There a book is.

→

3. There many are people.

→

4. There was your cars.

→

5. There are some money in his pocket.

→

6. There a table is.

→

7. There was three cats.

→

8. There many pens are.

→

9. There a notebook is.

→

10. There was two birds and one dog.

→

EXERCISE 2

다음 문장을 의문문과 부정문으로 만드세요

1. There is a book on the table.

→

→

2. There are three apples.

→

→

3. There is only one bed in my room.

→

→

4. There are many people.

→

→

5. There was a new watch under the chair.

→

→

6. There were a lot of pens in the pencil case.

→

→

7. There is much money in the envelope.

→

→

8. There are my daughters.

→

→

9. There are many cars.

→

→

10. There is a new watch.

→

→

1 밑줄 친 It 의 쓰임이 다른 것은?

① It is Friday today.
② It is a book.
③ It's nine o'clock on a Saturday.
④ It's still bright outside.
⑤ It was sunny yesterday.

2 다음 중 밑줄 친 부분이 어법상 틀린 것은?

① There is a library in my town.
② There are a desk in my room.
③ There are four cups on the table.
④ There are six boxes on the floor.
⑤ There is a post office near the market.

3 다음 밑줄 친 it의 쓰임과 같은 것은?

Is it Tuesday today?

① It's not yours.
② Is It in the box?
③ It isn't apple juice.
④ It snows in December.
⑤ It was a very exciting game.

4 다음 문장에서 어법상 틀린 것은?

There is three dogs on the sofa.
　① 　② 　③ 　④ 　　⑤

5 다음 빈칸에 공통으로 들어갈 말을 쓰세요.

_____ is fall here.
_____ is windy and rainy now.
_____ is Friday today.

6 다음 질문에 대한 대답으로 알맞은 것은?

A: Are there many students in your school?
B: _____

① Yes, they are.　② No, there are.
③ No, they aren't.　④ No, there aren't.
⑤ Yes, there aren't.

7 다음 우리말과 일치하도록 빈칸에 알맞은 말을 쓰세요.

탁자 위에 오렌지 하나가 있다.

→ _____ _____ _____ _____ on the table.

8 다음 중 밑줄 친 It의 쓰임이 나머지 넷과 다른 것은?

① It's my pet.
② It's dark here.
③ It's eight o'clock.
④ It's hot in summer
⑤ It's Thursday today.

9 다음 빈칸에 들어갈 말이 나머지 넷과 <u>다른</u> 것은?

① There_____an apple in the box.
② There_____two pens on the desk.
③ There____three cups on the shelf.
④ There_____red roses in the vase.
⑤ There_____many people in the mall.

10 다음 빈칸에 들어갈 말로 알맞지 <u>않은</u> 것은?

There is_____.

① lots of snow in winter.
② many flowers in the vase.
③ some money in my pocket.
④ little rain here in summer.
⑤ a ball in the box.

11 다음 우리말에 맞도록 빈칸에 공통으로 들어갈 알맞은 말을 쓰세요.

(1) 이 방 안이 매우 어둡다.
→_____is quite dark in this room.

(2) 오늘이 무슨 요일입니까?
→What day is_____today?

12 다음 빈칸에 들어갈 말로 알맞은 것을 고르세요.

The Earth is changing._____is getting hotter. This is because the air is getting dirtier and dirtier.

① It   ② This
③ That   ④ They
⑤ What

[13-15] 다음 주어진 단어들을 순서에 맞게 배열하세요.

13 the answer / is / there.

→ _____

14 the street / a car / is / there / on.

→ _____

15 the corner / your / there / is / umbrella / in.

→ _____

[16-17] 다음 주어진 단어들에서 필요한 단어들을 골라 순서에 맞게 배열하세요.

16 games / there / are / my / is / favorite.

→ _____

17 there / your / are / lunch / the table / on / is.

→ _____

Unit 10 조동사 can, may

- 조동사 기본사항

- 허락과 허가의 조동사 can, may

- 가능의 조동사 can

- 추측의 조동사 may

Gorilla Grammar

unit 10 조동사 can, may

1 조동사 기본 사항

a. 조동사 뒤에는 동사원형이 온다.
- She can plays the guitar. (X)
- She can play the guitar. (O)
  그녀는 기타를 칠 수 있다.

b. 접속사를 안 쓸 경우 한 문장에는 조동사 한 개만 사용한다.
- She will can do that. (x)
- She will be able to do that. (o)
  그녀는 그것을 할 수 있을 것이다.

c. 부정문과 의문문을 만들 때 조동사를 활용한다.
- She can doesn't play the piano. (X)
- She can't (cannot) play the piano. (O)
  그녀는 피아노를 연주할 수 없다.
- Can she play the piano? (O)
  그녀는 피아노를 연주할 수 있을까?

---- **Exercise 1** --

다음 문장에서 문법적으로 틀린 부분을 고치세요.

1. He can plays the guitar very well.
→

2. She may coming back tomorrow.
→

3. I will may meet you later.
→

4. May I going home?
→

5. Can I am back in time for the show?
→

---- **Exercise 1-1** --

다음 문장에서 문법적으로 틀린 부분을 고치세요.

1. Jane can does that by herself.
→

2. It cans not be true.
→

3. This movie may is boring for you.
→

4. May I wrote a letter with a red pen?
→

5. He can runs very fast.
→

unit 10 조동사 can, may

2 허락과 허가의 조동사 can, may

• 허락을 맡거나 허가를 내려줄 때 사용. may는 의문문에서 1인칭일 때만 사용.
may와 can은 서로 교체가능하다.

- Can(May) I open the door?

  문을 열어도 될까요?

- You can(may) go to the concert.

  너는 콘서트에 가도된다.

- You can(may) play computer games until midnight.

  너는 자정까지 컴퓨터 게임을 할 수 있다.

- Can you help me?

- May you help me? (x)

  너는 나를 도울 수 있니?

- Can(May) I eat the hamburger?

  햄버거를 먹어도 될까요?

- -Yes, you can(may). /No, you can't(may not).

  응, 그래. /아니, 안 돼.

---- **Exercise 1** --

다음 질문에 적절한 대답을 쓰세요.

1. May I come back tomorrow?

긍정 →

부정 →

2. Can I use your pen?

긍정 →

부정 →

3. Can I borrow your umbrella?

긍정 →

부정 →

4. May I go home?

긍정 →

부정 →

5. May I call you now?

긍정 →

부정 →

---- **Exercise 2** --

괄호 안의 단어를 참고하여 다음 문장을 영작하세요.

1. 제가 당신을 도와드릴까요? (may)

→

2. 제가 집에 가도 되나요? (may)

→

3. 제게 돈을 조금 빌려줄 수 있나요? (can, lend)

→

4. 당신은 언제든지 나에게 전화해도 됩니다. (can, anytime)

→

5. 제가 당신의 펜을 사용해도 될까요? (may)

→

6. 제가 메시지를 남겨도 될까요? (may, leave)

→

7. 당신은 나를 John이라고 불러도 됩니다. (can)

→

8. 내가 너의 집에 가도 되니? (may)

→

9. 제가 이 의자에 앉아도 될까요? (may)

→

10. 당신은 여기 주차해도 됩니다. (can, park)

→

unit 10 조동사 can, may

가능의 조동사 can

- 조동사 can은 가능의 의미로 '할 수 있다'로 해석될 수 있다.
- 가능의 조동사 can은 be able to 동사원형으로도 바꿀 수 있다.

- I can finish the report until tomorrow.

  나는 그 보고서를 내일까지 끝낼 수 있다.

- She is able to pass the exam.

  그녀는 시험을 통과할 수 있다.

- I can't help the girl.

  나는 그 소녀를 도울 수 없다.

추측의 조동사 may

- 조동사 may는 추측의 의미로 '아마~일지도 모르겠다'로 해석될 수 있다.

- She may be tired by now.

  그녀는 지금쯤 피곤할지도 모르겠다.

- He may change his mind.

  그는 그의 마음을 바꿀지도 모르겠다.

- She may not love him.

  그녀는 그를 사랑하지 않을 지도 모르겠다.

---- **Exercise 1** --

다음 주어진 문장을 영작하세요.

1. 그녀는 피아노를 칠 수 있다.

→

2. 나는 더 이상 공부를 할 수 없다. (any more)

→

3. 그는 자고 있을 지도 모른다.

→

4. 그는 아마도 선생님일지도 모른다.

→

5. 나는 더 이상 먹을 수 없다.

→

6. 그 소식은 사실이 아닐지도 모른다. (the news)

→

7. 나의 남자형제는 일본어를 할 수 있다.

→

8. 그 소문은 사실일지도 모른다. (the rumor)

→

Unit 11 조동사 must, have to

- must
- have to
- must와 have to의 부정문

Gorilla Grammar

unit 11 조동사 must, have to

1 must

a. 의무를 나타내는 must

- 중요성, 구속력 있는 의무를 나타낼 때 사용 '~해야만 한다'로 해석

- You must keep the rules.

  너는 규칙을 지켜야한다.

b. 강한 추측을 나타내는 must

- 큰 확신을 가지고 추측할 때 사용 '~임에 틀림없다'로 해석

- She must be sad.

  그녀는 슬픔에 틀림없다.

2 have to

a. 의무를 나타내는 have to

- '해야만 한다.'로 해석되며 must와 바꿔 쓸 수 있다.

- You must keep the rules.

≒ You have to keep the rules.

  너는 규칙을 지켜야만 한다.

- must가 좀 더 구속력을 가진다.

3 must와 have to의 부정문

a. must not: ~해서는 안 된다.

- You must not follow the guy because he seems dangerous.

  너는 그 남자를 따라서는 안 된다. 그는 위험해보이기 때문에

b. don't have to: ~할 필요가 없다.

- You don't have to follow the guy because I can help you.

  너는 그 남자를 따를 필요가 없다. 내가 도와줄 수 있기 때문에.

---- **Exercise 1** --

다음 주어진 문장을 주어진 단어를 활용하여 영작하세요.

1. 나는 지금 떠나야만 한다. (have to)

→

2. 그는 그의 숙제를 지금 당장 해야만 한다. (must)

→

3. 그녀는 혼자 사는 것이 틀림없다. (must)

→

4. 너는 집으로 돌아와야 한다. (have to)

→

5. 나는 내 이메일을 확인해야만 한다. (must, check)

→

---- **Exercise 1-1** --

다음 주어진 문장을 주어진 단어를 활용하여 영작하세요.

1. 그녀는 가난한 것이 틀림없다. (must)

→

2. 나는 오늘 그를 만나야만 한다. (have to)

→

3. 너는 내일 일찍 일어나야만 한다. (must)

→

4. 그 개는 배가 고픈 것이 틀림없다. (must)

→

5. 그녀는 집에 머물러야만 한다. (have to)

→

---- **Exercise 1-2** --

다음 주어진 문장을 영작하세요.

1. 너는 그것을 지금 할 필요가 없다.

→

2. 너는 그 차를 사서는 안 된다.

→

3. 너는 그 차를 살 필요가 없다.

→

4. 나는 그에게 소리쳐서는 안 된다. (yell at)

→

5. 그는 버스를 탈 필요가 없다.

→

---- **Exercise 1-3** --

다음 주어진 문장을 영작하세요.

1. 그녀는 이 책을 읽어야 한다.

→

2. 그는 나에게 돈을 빌려줄 필요가 없다. (lend)

→

3. 나는 피아노를 연주해야만 한다.

→

4. 나는 피아노를 연주해서는 안 된다.

→

5. 나는 피아노를 연주할 필요가 없다.

→

Unit 10 조동사 can, may   Unit 11 조동사 must, have to

1 다음 우리말에 맞도록 할 때 빈칸에 들어갈 말로 알맞은 것을 고르세요.

> 제가 내일 그와 함께해도 될까요?
> → _____ I come with him tomorrow?

① Will
② May
③ Must
④ Have
⑤ Should

2 다음 우리말에 맞도록 할 때 빈칸에 들어갈 말로 알맞은 것을 고르세요.

> 오후에 비가 올 지도 모른다.
> → It _____ rain in the afternoon.

① have to
② has to
③ must
④ will
⑤ may

3 다음 대화의 밑줄 친 부분과 바꿔 쓸 수 <u>없는</u> 것은?

> A: May I have some water?
> B: <u>Why not?</u>

① Yes, you may.   ② Of course.
③ Go ahead.   ④ Sure.
⑤ I'm afraid not.

4 다음 문장에서 not이 들어갈 위치로 알맞은 곳은?

> Jason (①) will (②) come (③) to (④) Tiffany's party (⑤) next week.

5 다음 빈칸에 들어갈 말로 알맞은 것은?

> She may _____ interested in math.

① is
② be
③ are
④ was
⑤ were

6 다음 우리말을 영어로 옮긴 것이 <u>틀린</u> 것은?

① 내가 여기서 머물러도 될까?
  Can I stay here?
② 그녀는 그 파티에 올 수 있다.
  She can come to the party.
③ 너는 들어와도 좋다.
  You may come in.
④ 너는 가서 그 영화를 보아야 한다.
  You must go and see that movie.
⑤ 제가 당신께 질문을 해도 되나요?
  Must I ask you a question?

7 다음 빈칸에 must를 쓸 수 <u>없는</u> 것은?

① I_____go now.
② She will_____lose weight.
③ The boy_____be very diligent.
④ He_____be a pilot.
⑤ You_____cross the street at a crosswalk.

8 다음 빈칸에 들어갈 말이 어법상 <u>틀린</u> 것은?

Jessica can_____.

① make bread
② drive a car
③ solve the math problem
④ plays the piano
⑤ help her friends

9 다음 우리말을 영어로 바르게 옮긴 것은?

그가 내일 그녀를 도와야 할까?

① He should helps her tomorrow?
② Should he help her tomorrow?
③ He helps should her tomorrow?
④ Should he helps her tomorrow?
⑤ Should help he her tomorrow?

10 다음 우리말에 맞도록 할 때 빈칸에 들어갈 말이 순서대로 짝지어진 것은?

Chris와 통화할 수 있을까요?
→_____ I speak to Chris?

제 대신 이 편지를 보내 주시겠어요?
→_____ you send this letter for me?

① May - Can
② Will - Should
③ Must - Can't
④ Will - Can
⑤ Should - Have to

11 다음 빈칸에 들어갈 말로 알맞지 <u>않은</u> 것은?

My son_____study hard.

① will
② can
③ must
④ have to
⑤ may

12 다음 밑줄 친 부분의 의미가 나머지와 <u>다른</u> 하나는?

① Hot water <u>may</u> keep us warm.
② You <u>may</u> use your pen.
③ <u>May</u> I take pictures here?
④ <u>May</u> I try this shirt on?
⑤ You <u>may</u> have a seat.

13 다음 밑줄 친 우리말을 영어로 바르게 옮긴 것은?

A: Will you go swimming with me tomorrow?
B: Sorry, <u>나는 수영을 못해</u>.

① I won't swim   ② I mustn't swim
③ I can't swim   ④ I shouldn't swim
⑤ I may not swim

14 다음 중 밑줄 친 부분과 바꿔 쓸 수 있는 것은?

You <u>have to</u> do your task right now. The boss is coming.

① must
② can
③ could
④ do
⑤ will

15 다음 문장을 부정문으로 바르게 고친 것은?

I can build a big snowman.

① I will build a big snowman.
② I can't build a big snowman.
③ I can no build a big snowman.
④ I not can build a big snowman.
⑤ I am able to build a big snowman,

16 다음 대화의 빈칸에 공동으로 들어갈 알맞은 말을 모두 고르세요.

A: _____ I sit here?
B: Yes, you_____.

① M(m)ust
② C(c)an
③ S(s)hould
④ M(m)ay
⑤ W(w)ill

17 다음 우리말을 영어로 바르게 옮긴 것은?

나는 오늘 편지를 부칠 필요가 없어.

① I must not send the letter today.
② I could not send the letter today.
③ I may send the letter today.
④ I had not to send the letter today.
⑤ I don't have to send the letter today.

18 다음 문장에서 틀린 부분을 찾아 바르게 고쳐 쓰세요.

Tom will does the dishes after dinner.
→ _____.

19 다음 두 문장의 뜻이 일치하도록 빈칸에 알맞은 말을 쓰세요.

> She can make a cake.
> → She_____ _____ _____make a cake.

20 다음 밑줄 친 단어와 바꿔도 의미가 변하지 않는 것을 고르세요.

> May I take your order?

① Must
② Can
③ Should
④ have to
⑤ Will

21 다음 중 밑줄 친 <u>must</u>의 의미가 나머지 넷과 다른 것은?

① She <u>must</u> go to school.
② She <u>must</u> be sad because of the news.
③ She <u>must</u> clean your room.
④ She <u>must</u> help your parents.
⑤ She <u>must</u> go to bed early.

22 다음 두 문장의 의미가 <u>다른</u> 것은?

① He will come at 8 a.m.
  → He is going to come at 8 a.m.
② Can you play tennis?
  → Are you able to play tennis?
③ You can go home now.
  → You may go home now.
④ You must not sleep here.
  → You don't have to sleep here.
⑤ My uncle can make pizza.
  → My uncle is able to make pizza.

Unit **12** 감각동사

Gorilla Grammar

unit 12 감각동사

• 2형식 동사 중에 '감각동사'는 뒤에 보어로 형용사만이 온다.

감각동사	feel (~하게 느끼다), look (~하게 보이다), sound (~하게 들리다), smell (~한 냄새가 나다), taste (~한 맛이 나다)

• You look great.

너는 멋져 보인다.

• The soup tastes salty.

그 스프는 짠 맛이 난다.

• This perfume smells good.

이 향수는 좋은 냄새가 난다.

• He felt hungry.

그는 배고픈 것을 느꼈다.

• His plan sounds perfect.

그의 계획은 완벽한 것처럼 들린다.

- -

★ 참고) 형용사: '~ㄴ'으로 보통 해석된다.

pretty, smart, beautiful, upset, hungry, kind, sleepy, delicious, difficult, young, tall 등

★ 보어로 명사를 쓰고 싶다면 'like'와 함께 쓰면 된다.

• She looks like an angel.

그녀는 천사인 것처럼 보인다

• This perfume smells like a watermelon.

이 향수는 수박같은 냄새가 난다.

---- **Exercise 1** --

다음 문장을 괄호 안의 감각동사를 활용하여 영작하세요.

1. 그녀는 아름다워 보인다. (look)

→

2. 이 음식은 맛있다. (taste)

→

3. 그녀는 행복을 느꼈다. (feel)

→

4. 김치에서 매운 냄새가 난다. (smell, spicy)

→

5. 그거 훌륭하네! (sound)

→

6. 이 빵은 냄새가 나쁘다. (smell)

→

7. 그 방은 깨끗해 보인다. (look)

→

8. 이 초는 좋은 냄새가 난다. (smell)

→

---- **Exercise 1-1** --

다음 문장을 괄호 안의 감각동사를 활용하여 영작하세요.

1. 그 파이는 맛있어 보인다. (pie, look)

→

2. 그 피자는 좋은 냄새가 난다. (smell)

→

3. 그것은 좋게 들린다. (sound)

→

4. 나는 상쾌함을 느꼈다. (fresh)

→

5. 그녀는 예뻐 보인다. (look)

→

6. 너는 모델처럼 보인다. (look like)

→

7. 이것은 일본 음식 같은 냄새가 난다. (smell like)

→

8. 이것은 피자 같은 맛이 난다. (taste like)

→

Unit 13 4형식 동사

- 4형식
- 4형식을 3형식으로 전환

Gorilla Grammar

unit 13 4형식 동사

1 4형식

4형식 문장	주어 + 동사 + 간접목적어 (~에게) + 직접목적어 (을/를)

4형식 동사들
give, make, lend, send, show, tell, buy, write, cook 등

- I gave him a present.
  나는 그에게 선물 하나를 주었다.
- She made me a cake.
  그녀는 나에게 케이크 하나를 만들어 주었다.
- They showed him the pictures.
  그들은 그에게 사진들을 보여주었다.

2 4형식을 3형식으로 전환

- 4형식 문장을 간접목적어와 직접목적어의 위치를 바꾸고 그 사이에 알맞은 전치사를 넣음으로써 3형식 문장으로 바꿔 쓸 수 있다.

4형식 문장 주어 + 동사 +	간접목적어 + 직접목적어
↓	
3형식 문장 주어 + 동사 +	직접목적어 + 전치사 + 간접목적어

- -

★ 전치사 고르기

of	ask 등
for	buy, make, get, find, cook 등
to	tell, give, lend, send 등

unit 13 4형식 동사

- I gave him a present.

  → I gave a present **to** him.

  나는 그에게 선물 하나를 주었다.

- She made me a cake.

  → She made a cake **for** me.

  그녀는 나에게 케이크 하나를 만들어 주었다.

- He asked me her birthday.

  → He asked her birthday **of** me.

  그는 나에게 그녀의 생일을 물었다.

---- **Exercise 1** ---

다음 4형식 문장을 3형식 문장으로 바꾸세요.

1. She gave me a book.

→

2. I tell him the truth.

→

3. I bought her a pair of earrings.

→

4. Jane wrote me a letter.

→

5. I made you a cake.

→

6. He sometimes lends her some money.

→

7. He sent me an e-mail.

→

8. They showed us something funny.

→

---- **Exercise 1-1** --

다음 4형식은 3형식으로, 3형식은 4형식 문장으로 바꾸세요.

1. We can tell you something special.

→

2. She gave me some books.

→

3. He asked her our vacation plan.

→

4. I can teach English to you.

→

5. She showed me her diary.

→

6. Mom made a new dress for me.

→

7. She wrote an e-mail to us.

→

8. I bought a cell phone for her.

→

Unit 14　문장의 종류

- 문장의 종류
- 문장의 구성

Gorilla Grammar

unit 14 문장의 종류

문장의 종류

- 1형식: 주어 + 동사 _(주인공)
  명+은/는/이/가
- 2형식: 주어 + 동사 + 주격 보어 _(보충어) 명/형
- 3형식: 주어 + 동사 + 목적어 명+을/를
- 4형식: 주어 + 동사 + 간접목적어 + 직접목적어
- 5형식: 주어 + 동사 + 목적어 + 목적 보어
  ~에게   ~을/를

문장의 구성

• 문장을 구성하는 단어의 역할을 살펴보자.

- 명사: 주어, 목적어, 보어
- 동사: 동사
- 형용사: 보어, 명사 수식
- 부사: 문장 구성 안 함. 명사를 제외하고 다 수식

용어설명

★ 주어: 문장의 주인공

★ 보어: 보충어

　주격보어: 주어를 보충설명

　목적격보어: 목적어를 보충설명

★ 참고: 전치사 + 명사 = 부사

---- **Exercise 1** --

다음 문장의 형식을 말하고 해석하세요.

1. My mom bought me new pants.

→

2. My mom bought new pants.

→

3. The milk went bad.

→

4. I will marry you.

→

5. I am a boy.

→

6. I made this cake.

→

7. The plan sounds fun.

→

8. She showed me a ring.

→

9. The leaves turned green.

→

10. She made him a lawyer.

→

다음 문장의 형식을 말하고 해석하세요.

1. They call me Bunny.

→

2. She usually goes to bed late.

→

3. I fixed the computer.

→

4. The sun rises in the east.

→

5. He fell asleep easily.

→

6. We named the girl Jane.

→

7. I take a bath every day.

→

8. I wanted your bag yesterday.

→

9. Jane gave me some money in front of her house.

→

---- **Exercise 1-2** --

다음 문장의 형식을 말하고 해석하세요.

1. My brother is tall.

→

2. An apple is on the desk.

→

3. He often tells me a funny story.

→

4. He looks handsome.

→

5. The game is not easy.

→

6. They teach me English twice a week.

→

7. She became a doctor.

→

8. I cried hard yesterday.

→

9. They are in the room.

→

---- **Exercise 1-3** --

다음 문장의 형식을 말하고 해석하세요.

1. I run every day.

→

2. We called him John at the bar.

→

3. He made me a dentist.

→

4. I wrote a letter with all my heart.

→

5. I make a box for you.

→

6. I had dinner with him.

→

7. She makes me happy.

→

8. You don't look happy today.

→

9. I sometimes play the piano.

→

10. You are really pretty.

→

1 다음 빈칸에 들어갈 말로 알맞지 <u>않은</u> 것은?

You look_____today.

① happy
② angry
③ nice
④ sadly
⑤ wonderful

2 다음 중 어법상 <u>틀린</u> 문장은?

① You look blue.
② The pizza tastes delicious.
③ The soap smells sweet.
④ It sounds awesome.
⑤ He feels happily.

3 다음 문장에서 <u>틀린</u> 부분을 찾아 바르게 고쳐 쓰세요.

The candy tastes sweetly.

_____ → _____

4 다음 우리말을 영어로 바르게 옮긴 것은?

그 야채들은 신선해 보인다.

① The vegetables are fresh.
② The vegetables looks fresh.
③ The vegetables look freshly.
④ The vegetables look fresh.
⑤ The vegetables doesn't look fresh.

5 다음 우리말과 일치하도록 주어진 단어를 사용하여 영어로 옮기세요.

너의 손은 차갑게 느껴진다. (cold)
→ _____.

6 다음 빈칸에 들어갈 말로 알맞지 <u>않은</u> 것은?

He looks_____.

① happy
② good
③ friendly
④ smart
⑤ interestingly

7 다음 대화의 흐름이 자연스럽게 연결되도록 괄호 안의 단어들을 바르게 배열한 것은?

A: You look happy.
B: Yes I'm so happy because my mother bought_____.
(my/ a computer/ me/ birthday/ for)

① a computer for me my birthday
② a computer me for my birthday
③ my a computer for me birthday
④ me a computer for my birthday
⑤ for me a computer my birthday

8. 다음 대화를 완성하세요.

A: Who gave you a sandwich?
B: My friend Lisa gave it _____ me.

9 우리말과 일치하도록 주어진 말을 바르게 배열 한 것은?

우진이는 미나에게 펜을 주었다.
ⓐ Woojin ⓑ a pen ⓒ Mina ⓓ gave

① ⓐ - ⓓ - ⓑ - ⓒ
② ⓐ - ⓑ - ⓓ - ⓒ
③ ⓒ - ⓑ - ⓐ - ⓓ
④ ⓐ - ⓓ - ⓒ - ⓑ
⑤ ⓒ - ⓑ - ⓓ - ⓐ

10 다음 빈칸에 들어갈 말로 알맞지 <u>않은</u> 것을 고르세요.

Mr.Kim_____us a comic book.

① gave
② lent
③ bought
④ sent
⑤ liked

11 다음 중 문장의 형식이 다른 하나는?

① She cooked them pasta.
② Anna baked me cookies.
③ He built a house for his family.
④ They asked the teacher private questions.
⑤ Jack bought her some books.

12 다음 빈칸에 들어갈 말이 순서대로 바르게 짝지어진 것은?

He bought a pizza_____us.
She sent a letter_____me.

① to - to
② for - for
③ at - to
④ of - for
⑤ for - to

[13-14] 다음 주어진 문장을 영작하고 몇 형식인지도 밝히세요.

13 그 사건이 그를 강하게 만들었다. (the accident)

→ _____

14 그 계획은 합리적으로 들린다. (rational)

→ _____

15 다음 중 문장이 문법에 맞게 구성되도록 올바른 것을 고르세요.

(1) She always sleeps (deep /deeply).

(2) The cake looks (sweet /sweetly).

16 다음 중 어법상 <u>틀린</u> 문장은?

① She made him sadly.
② He entered the room.
③ She sent me a card.
④ They bought a shirt for him.
⑤ She cried all day.

[17-19] 다음 주어진 문장에서 어법상 틀린 것을 찾아 고치세요.

17 Him cooked bulgogi to me.

18 They showed beautiful pictures her.

19 The seasoning makes food spicily.

20 4형식의 문장을 3형식으로 바꿀 때 전치사 for을 쓰는 동사들을 3개 이상 쓰세요.

_____

Unit 15 to부정사를 목적어로 하는 동사

Gorilla Grammar

unit 15 to부정사를 목적어로 하는 동사

- 목적어 자리에는 명사가 온다. 하지만 명사역할을 하는 to 부정사나 동명사도 올 수 있다. 여기에선 to 부정사를 목적어로 하는 동사를 배우도록 한다.

<table>
<tr><td>to 부정사를 목적어로 하는 동사
want, hope, like, start, try, decide, learn 등</td></tr>
</table>

- I hope to meet the girl.
  그 소녀를 만나길 희망한다.
- I decided to make a reservation.
  나는 예약하기로 결심했다.
- I started to grow the plant.
  나는 식물을 기르기 시작했다.

★ 단, 위의 like, start 그리고 try는 동명사(동사ing) 와도 함께 쓸 수 있다는 점을 기억해라.

---- **Exercise 1** --

다음 문장에서 어색한 부분을 찾아서 고치세요.

1. I started save money.

2. Does she learn cook?

3. He really to like to run in the morning.

4. She decided quitting the job.

5. I am hoping leave for France soon.

6. They want staying here.

7. I to decided to wait for him.

8. Do you like drink at the pub?

9. Do we to start to make a plan?

10. She hopes meeting them.

---- **Exercise 1-1** --

다음 문장에서 어색한 부분을 찾아서 고치세요.

1. Does she to like to play the piano?

2. They decided to gave her a present.

3. I am hoping to seeing her soon.

4. Did you try to talked with him?

5. She learned dancing together.

6. He decided clean the room.

7. I started to taking a yoga lesson.

8. We want playing soccer.

9. They decided go to the movies.

10. Do you want take an exam?

---- **Exercise 2** --

다음 문장을 보기의 단어를 활용하여 영작하세요.

1. 나는 미국에 방문하기를 희망한다.(hope)

→

2. 나는 낮잠 자는 것을 좋아한다.(take a nap)

→

3. 그는 그의 일을 하기 시작한다.(start)

→

4. 영어로 말하도록 해보세요.(try, in English)

→

5. 나는 일찍 일어나기를 원한다. (want)

→

6. 그녀는 나와 춤을 추고 싶어 한다.(like)

→

7. 비가 오기 시작한다. (start)

→

8. 너는 그를 만나고 싶니? (want)

→

9. 나는 이 셔츠를 입기 싫다. (like, shirt)

→

10. 나는 내 시계를 찾으려 노력하고 있다. (try)

→

---- **Exercise 2-1** --

다음 문장을 보기의 단어를 활용하여 영작하세요.

1. 나는 뭔가를 먹고 싶다. (want)

→

2. 그녀는 큰소리로 말하려고 노력한다. (speak up)

→

3. 그들은 창문 닦는 것을 좋아하지 않는다. (like)

→

4. 그는 이기기를 희망한다. (hope)

→

5. 우리는 과일들을 먹기 시작했다. (start)

→

6. 나는 일찍 떠나기 싫다. (want)

→

7. 그들은 지금 멈추는 것을 좋아하지 않는다. (like)

→

8. 그녀는 강에서 수영하는 것을 좋아한다. (like)

→

9. 영어로 생각하도록 노력해라. (try to, in English)

→

10. 나는 그 팀에 참여하려고 노력한다. (join)

→

Unit 16 지각동사, 사역동사

- 지각동사와 사역동사

- 지각동사와 사역동사의 종류

Gorilla Grammar

unit 16 지각동사, 사역동사

1 지각동사와 사역동사

- **지각동사:** 감각기관을 통해서 대상을 인식하는 동사
- **사역동사:** '시키고', '하게 한다'라는 의미의 동사

2 지각동사와 사역동사의 종류

지각동사	watch (지켜보다), see (보다), feel (느끼다), hear (듣다) 등
사역동사	make, let, have (시키다, 하게하다)

a. 지각동사는 뒤에 동사원형이나 동사원형ing가 온다.

b. 사역동사는 뒤에 동사원형이 온다.

c. 지각동사나 사역동사가 아닐 경우 뒤에 to 부정사가 온다. (예외있음)

- I want him to clean his room.

  나는 그가 그의 방을 청소하길 원한다.

- I made him clean his room.

  나는 그가 그의 방을 청소하게 했다.

- I watched him cleaning(clean) his room.

  나는 그가 그의 방을 청소하는 것을 지켜봤다.

---- **Exercise 1** --

다음 문장에서 문법적으로 틀린 부분을 고치고 해석하세요.

1. I want you pass the exam.

→

2. I saw her to play the guitar.

→

3. My mom made me to clean the room.

→

4. He felt her touched his shoulder.

→

5. I will let him to know the truth.

→

6. She persuaded me buy the product.

→

7. He let me lying to my mother.

→

8. Let me to go there.

→

9. Can you make him brought the box?

→

10. They heard her to cry.

→

---- **Exercise 1-1** ---

다음 문장에서 문법적으로 틀린 부분을 고치고 해석하세요.

1. I heard the teacher to shout at the students.

→

2. I made her to wash the dishes.

→

3. Tom saw him played the piano.

→

4. They want me sing a song.

→

5. She watches him to draw a picture.

→

6. The police doesn't see the woman left the bank.

→

7. She makes me to find her wallet.

→

8. We heard birds to sing.

→

9. She let me doing it.

→

10. Jane made me crying.

→

---- **Exercise 2** --

다음 괄호 안의 단어를 이용하여 영작하세요.

1. 그는 그의 아들이 왕이 되길 원한다. (want)

→

2. 그는 그녀가 그 소설을 읽고 있는 것을 보았다. (watch, novel)

→

3. 그녀는 나를 웃게 만든다. (make, laugh)

→

4. 우리는 그가 친절하게 되길 원한다. (want, kind)

→

5. 나는 그가 숙제를 하게 했다. (have)

→

6. 나는 그녀가 방에 들어가는 것을 봤다. (see)

→

7. 그들은 무언가가 뒤에 서있다고 느꼈다. (feel, stand behind the back)

→

8. 그는 그녀가 노래를 부르고 있는 것을 들었다. (hear)

→

9. 그녀는 내가 방에 들어가는 것을 봤다. (watch, enter)

→

10. 그들은 내가 그에게 전화 걸게 만들었다. (have, call)

→

---- **Exercise 2-1** --

다음 괄호 안의 단어를 이용하여 영작하세요.

1. 나는 그가 그 상자를 운반하기를 원한다. (want, carry)

→

2. 그녀는 그가 그 의자를 팔도록 설득했다. (persuade, sell)

→

3. 나는 내 아들이 걷는 것을 보았다. (see)

→

4. 그들은 그가 운전하도록 시켰다. (have, drive)

→

5. 나는 네가 자러가길 원한다. (want, go to sleep)

→

6. 우리는 그가 그녀를 초대하도록 강요했다. (force, invite)

→

7. 그는 누군가가 우는 것을 느꼈다. (feel)

→

8. 나는 그가 그녀를 향해 소리치는 것을 들었다. (hear, yell at)

→

9. 그녀는 그가 그 책을 읽도록 허락했다. (let)

→

10. 나는 그 아기가 우는 것을 들었다. (hear)

→

Unit 17 접속사 that

Gorilla Grammar

unit 17 접속사 that

- 명사절 that은 뒤에 완전한 문장이 와서 '~라는 것'으로 해석되어 명사처럼
  주어, 목적어, 보어자리에 들어간다. 여기에서는 목적어역할 위주로 공부하자.

- I believe that he is innocent.

  나는 믿는다 그가 결백하다는 것을.
- They think that she isn't pretty.

  그들은 생각한다 그녀가 예쁘지 않다는 것을.
- He hopes that his son will be a lawyer.

  그는 희망한다 그의 아들이 변호사가 되리라는 것은.
- I know that I am not stupid.

  나는 안다 내가 멍청하지 않다는 것을.

---- **Exercise 1** --

다음 주어진 문장을 영작하세요.

1. 나는 안다 그가 잘생겼다는 것을.

→

2. 나는 믿는다 그녀가 화나지 않았다는 것을.

→

3. 나는 생각한다 그가 잘생겼다는 것을

→

4. 나는 희망한다 그녀가 행복해지기를.

→

5. 그녀는 말했다 그 방이 어두웠다는 것을.

→

---- **Exercise 1-1** --

다음 주어진 문장을 영작하세요.

1. 그는 안다 그녀가 슬프다는 것을.

→

2. 그녀는 믿는다 그가 정말 바빴다는 것을.

→

3. 나는 말했다 그가 그녀를 좋아했다는 것을.

→

4. 그들은 생각했다 그가 재미있다고.

→

5. 우리는 희망했다 그가 돌아올 것을.

→

Unit **18** 접속사 because, when

- because

- when

Gorilla Grammar

unit 18 접속사 because, when

because

a. because : '왜냐하면'으로 해석. because 뒤에 원인을 나타내는 절이 온다.

- She was angry, because he was late.

  그녀는 화가 났었다 왜냐하면 그가 늦었기 때문에.

- She studies hard, because she wants to be a doctor.

  그녀는 열심히 공부한다 왜냐하면 의사가 되고 싶기 때문에.

when

a. when: '~할 때'로 해석.

- When he was young, he was smart.

  그가 어렸을 때, 그는 똑똑했다.

- I was young when I met her for the first time.

  나는 어렸다 내가 그녀를 처음으로 만났을 때.

---- **Exercise 1** --

빈칸에 because와 when 중 적절한 것을 넣으세요.

1. The weather was fine (   ) they went to the library.

2. Don't look down on him (   ) he is very smart.

3. Jane is always busy (   ) she has a lot of things to do.

4. They were going to Itaewon (   ) I called them.

5. I touched it (   ) I was curious.

6. Could you give me a call (   ) you wake up?

7. He could go out with her (   ) she didn't refuse.

8. I trust her (   ) she is honest.

9. I love her (   ) she is so beautiful.

10. I'll be there (   ) you finish your work.

---- **Exercise 1-1** --

빈칸에 because와 when 중 적절한 것을 넣고 해석하세요.

1. You always call me (　　　　　　　) I am busy.

2. She may run fast (　　　　　　) she is tall.

3. He joined the gang (　　　　　　) he was 15 years old.

4. I don't think he is a suspect (　　　　　　) he has an alibi.

5. Call me (　　　　　) you are free.

6. You can't leave simply (　　　　　　) you are tired.

7. I was upset (　　　　　) he ignored me.

8. She is so popular at her school (　　　　　　) she is beautiful.

9. I cannot smell anything (　　　　　) I have a stuffy nose.

10. We will go to the mall (　　　　　) I have something to buy.

---- **Exercise 2** --

다음 문장을 because나 when을 사용하여 영작하세요.

1. 그는 어렸을 때 키가 컸다.

→

2. 나는 점심을 안 먹었기 때문에 지금 배가 고프다.

→

3. 나는 부자가 아니기 때문에 그 차를 살 수 없다.

→

4. 나는 부자이기 때문에 그 집을 살 수 있다.

→

5. 집에 도착하면 나에게 전화해다오.

→

6. 그가 문을 두드릴 때 나는 방에서 노래를 하고 있었다.

→

7. 그는 키가 크기 때문에 농구를 잘한다.

→

8. 그녀는 매우 예뻐서 우리 마을에서 유명해졌다.

→

9. 나는 오늘 바쁘지 않아서 너를 만날 수 있다.

→

10. 그녀는 고등학교에 다닐 때 공부를 열심히 했다.

→

1 다음 빈칸에 들어갈 알맞은 말을 모두 고르세요.

> She saw him_____ his classroom.

① to clean
② clean
③ cleaned
④ to cleaning
⑤ cleaning

2 다음 빈칸에 들어갈 알맞은 말을 고르세요.

> The doctor decided_____every day for his health.

① exercise
② exercised
③ exercising
④ to exercise
⑤ to exercised

3 다음 문장 중 어법 상 잘못된 것은?

① The students enjoyed cleaning the classroom.
② My little brother started making a robot.
③ Harry finished reading a novel.
④ Do you mind opening the window?
⑤ She didn't want writing a letter.

4 다음 빈칸에 공통으로 들어갈 말로 알맞은 것은?

> I _____play basketball.
> I'd_____drink coffee.

① like
② likes
③ liking
④ like to
⑤ liking to

5 다음 우리말과 일치하도록 주어진 단어를 배열하세요.

> 그들은 케이크를 먹는 것을 좋아한다.
> (eat / they / like / to / cake)

→ _____

6 다음 밑줄 친 부분의 알맞은 형태는?

> He wants living in Busan.

① live
② lives
③ to live
④ living
⑤ to living

Unit 18 접속사 because, when

7 다음 빈칸에 들어갈 말로 알맞지 <u>않은</u> 것은?

> I_____to play baseball.

① love
② plan
③ want
④ enjoy
⑤ decide

8 다음 문장의 빈칸에 들어갈 말로 알맞은 것을 고르세요.

> I heard the man _____a song.

① to sing
② being singing
③ being sung
④ sing
⑤ sung

9 다음 문장의 빈칸에 들어갈 말로 알맞은 것을 고르세요.

> He let me_____soccer in the yard.

① to play
② playing
③ played
④ be played
⑤ play

10 다음 문장의 빈칸에 들어갈 말로 알맞지 <u>않은</u> 것을 고르세요.

> He would _____my kids to go outside.

① let
② want
③ tell
④ ask
⑤ order

11 다음 두 문장을 한 문장으로 만들 때, 빈칸에 들어갈 말로 알맞은 것을 모두 고르세요.

> I saw the boys. They were riding their bikes.
> → I saw the boys_____their bikes.

① rode
② riding
③ ride
④ to ride
⑤ ridden

12 주어진 말과 일치하도록 괄호 안의 말을 배열하세요.

> 나는 그가 잔디에 누워있는 것을 보았다.
> (on the grass / I / lying / saw / him)

→ _____

13 다음 문장의 빈칸에 들어갈 말로 알맞지 <u>않은</u> 것을 고르세요.

Thomas will_____me drink some wine.

① make
② let
③ see
④ watch
⑤ allow

14 다음 문장의 빈칸에 알맞은 말이 순서대로 짝지어진 것은?

I will let you_____how it works.
I felt the desk _____.

① knowing - shaking
② know - shake
③ to know - to shake
④ to know - shaking
⑤ knowing - shake

15 다음 문장에서 어법상 틀린 부분을 찾아 바르게 고쳐 쓰세요.

He made us to go home early.

_____

16 다음 문장의 빈칸에 들어갈 말의 알맞은 형태를 고르세요.

We made the children _____ their homework.

① doing
② did
③ done
④ do
⑤ be done

17 다음 문장의 빈칸에 들어갈 말의 알맞은 형태를 고르세요.

She made _____.

① clean the room us
② us clean the room
③ us the room clean
④ us to clean the room
⑤ us cleaning the room

Unit 18 접속사 because, when

[18-19] 다음 우리말을 영어로 옮길 때 빈칸에 들어갈 알맞은 말을 고르세요.

18

> 그는 피곤했기 때문에 파티에 가지 않았다.
> He didn't go to the party_____he was tired.

① and   ② because
③ if   ④ that
⑤ when

19

> 내가 힘들 때, 그녀는 나를 항상 도와준다.
> _____I am in trouble, she always helps me.

① And   ② Because
③ If   ④ That
⑤ When

20 주어진 문장의 밑줄 친 부분과 쓰임이 같은 것은?

> He knows <u>that</u> it's easy.

① Is <u>that</u> your book?
② <u>That</u>'s my house.
③ This is bigger than <u>that</u>.
④ I believe <u>that</u> he will be alive.
⑤ What is <u>that</u> small thing?

Unit 19 비교급 및 최상급

─────────────────

- 비교급과 최상급 만들기

Gorilla Grammar

unit 19 비교급 및 최상급

1 비교급과 최상급 만들기

비교 변화란 둘 또는 셋 이상 사물의 성질을 비교할 때 형용사와 부사의 형태가 변화하는 것을 말한다.

a. 규칙변화

	형용사 / 부사	비교급	최상급
1음절: -er, -est *-e로 끝나는 단어: -r, -st	smart	smarter	smartest
	young	younger	youngest
	wise	wiser	wisest
<단모음+단자음>로 끝나는 단어: 자음을 한 번 더 쓰고 -er, -est	big	bigger	biggest
	sad	sadder	saddest
	hot	hotter	hottest
<자음+y>로 끝나는 단어: -y → -ier, iest	pretty	prettier	prettiest
	happy	happier	happiest
3음절 이상이거나 -ful, -ous, -ing,-ish 등으로 끝나는 단어: 앞에 more, most를 붙인다.	careful	more careful	most careful
	famous	more famous	most famous
	surprising	more surprising	most surprising

b. 불규칙변화

형용사 / 부사	비교급	의미	최상급	의미
good /well	better	더 좋은	best	최고의
ill /bad	worse	더 나쁜	worst	최악의
many /much	more	더	most	가장, 최대의
little	less	덜	least	가장 적은, 최소의

EXERCISE 1

다음 주어진 단어의 비교급과 최상급을 만드세요.

1. tall → _____ _____

2. hot → _____ _____

3. pretty → _____ _____

4. famous → _____ _____

5. beautiful → _____ _____

다음 주어진 단어의 비교급과 최상급을 만드세요.

1. big → _____ _____

2. short → _____ _____

3. early → _____ _____

4. kind → _____ _____

5. useful → _____ _____

---- **Exercise 1-2** --

다음 주어진 단어의 비교급과 최상급을 만드세요.

1. old   →   _____   _____

2. good   →   _____   _____

3. ill   →   _____   _____

4. many   →   _____   _____

5. cute   →   _____   _____

---- **Exercise 1-3** --

다음 주어진 단어의 비교급과 최상급을 만드세요.

1. young   →   _____   _____

2. foolish   →   _____   _____

3. well   →   _____   _____

4. much   →   _____   _____

5. bad   →   _____   _____

2 비교급과 최상급 사용하기

a. 형용사 /부사의 비교급 + than: ~보다 더 ~하다

- Sophie is prettier than her sister.

  Sophie는 그녀의 여자형제보다 더 예쁘다.

- Mindy is more famous than her husband.

  Mindy는 그녀의 남편보다 더 유명하다.

b. the + 형용사 /부사의 최상급 (+ 명사) + 전치사 + 명사: ~에서 가장 ~한(하게)

- Sophie is the prettiest among her sisters.

  Sophie는 자매들 중에서 가장 예쁘다.

- Sophie is the prettiest girl in the office.

  Sophie는 사무실에서 가장 예쁜 여자이다.

---- **Exercise 1** ---

다음 문장을 괄호 안의 단어를 참고하여 영작하세요.

1. 그녀는 나보다 키가 크다. (tall)

→

2. 그는 그의 학급에서 가장 키가 크다. (tall / class)

→

3. 나는 너보다 나이가 많다. (old)

→

4. 오늘은 어제보다 덥다. (hot)

→

5. 이 영화는 저것보다 재미있다. (interesting)

→

6. 그는 나보다 강하다. (strong)

→

7. 이 집은 저 집보다 크다. (big)

→

8. 영어는 수학보다 어렵다. (difficult)

→

9. 나는 너보다 행복하다. (happy)

→

10. 펜이 연필보다 유용하다. (useful)

→

---- **Exercise 1-1** --

다음 문장을 괄호 안의 단어를 참고하여 영작하세요.

1. 너의 꿈이 가장 중요하다. (important)

→

2. 수학은 영어보다 쉽다. (easy)

→

3. 영화는 책보다 재미있다. (interesting)

→

4. 나는 그녀보다 현명하다. (wise)

→

5. 이 방은 저 방보다 크다. (large)

→

6. 오늘은 어제보다 따뜻하다. (warm)

→

7. 그는 나보다 행복하다. (happy)

→

8. 나는 너보다 젊다. (young)

→

9. 차는 자전거보다 빠르다. (fast)

→

10. 그는 그녀보다 똑똑하다. (smart)

→

---- **Exercise 1-2** --

다음 문장을 괄호 안의 단어를 참고하여 영작하세요.

1. 제주도는 한국에서 가장 큰 섬이다. (large)

→

2. 사랑이 내 삶에 가장 중요한 것이다. (important)

→

3. 그는 그의 반에서 가장 키가 크다. (tall)

→

4. 그녀는 그의 반에서 가장 어리다. (young)

→

5. 이 의자는 세상에서 제일 편안한 의자다. (comfortable)

→

6. 그녀는 그들 중에 가장 예쁘다. (pretty)

→

7. 이 휴대폰이 이 가게에서 가장 비싸다. (expensive)

→

8. 수학은 나에게 가장 어려운 과목이다. (difficult)

→

9. 나의 형은 우리 집에서 가장 힘이 센 남자다. (strong)

→

10. 이 상자는 우리 집에서 가장 큰 상자다. (big)

→

EXERCISE 1

---- **Exercise 1-3** --

다음 문장을 괄호 안의 단어를 참고하여 영작하세요.

1. 이 책은 이 도서관에서 가장 재미있는 책이다. (interesting)

→

2. 그녀는 이 세상에서 가장 행복한 여자다. (happy)

→

3. 이 방이 이 호텔에서 가장 큰 방이다. (large)

→

4. 이 책은 우리 집에서 가장 비싼 물건이다. (expensive)

→

5. Tom은 우리 반에서 가장 키가 큰 소년이다. (tall)

→

6. Jane은 우리 학교에서 가장 아름다운 소녀다. (beautiful)

→

7. 건강이 너의 삶에서 가장 중요한 것이다. (important)

→

8. 이 강은 세계에서 가장 긴 강이다. (long)

→

9. 그 남자는 뉴욕에서 가장 잘 생긴 남자다. (handsome)

→

10. 철(iron)이 그것들 중에서 가장 유용하다. (useful)

→

Unit 20 부가의문문

- 긍정문, 부정형 부가의문문

- 부정문, 긍정형 부가의문문

Gorilla Grammar

unit 20 부가의문문

1 긍정문, 부정형 부가의문문 : 그렇지 않니?

긍정문, be/do/조동사의 부정 축약형 + 주어(대명사) ?

- **She is intelligent, isn't she?** 그녀는 똑똑해, 그렇지 않니?
  - Yes, she is. 응, 똑똑해.
  - No, she isn't. 아니, 안 똑똑해.

- **She can help him, can't she?** 그녀는 그를 도울 수 있어, 그렇지 않니?
  - Yes, she can. 응, 도울 수 있어.
  - No, she can't. 아니, 도울 수 없어.

- **They are tall, aren't they?** 그들은 키가 커, 그렇지 않니?
  - Yes, they are. 응, 키가 커.
  - No, they aren't. 아니, 키가 안 커.

2 부정문, 긍정형 부가의문문: 그렇지?

부정문, be/do/조동사의 긍정형 + 주어(대명사) ?

- **She doesn't have a cat, does she?** 그녀는 고양이를 가지고 있지 않아, 그렇지?
  - Yes, she does. 아니, 가지고 있어.
  - No, she doesn't. 응, 안 가지고 있어.

- **She didn't have much money, did she?** 그녀는 많은 돈이 없었어, 그렇지?
  - Yes, she did. 아니, 있었어.
  - No, she didn't. 응, 없었어.

- **He can't dance, can he?** 그는 춤을 못 춰, 그렇지?
  - Yes, he can. 아니, 춰.
  - No, he can't. 응, 못 춰.

---- **Exercise 1** --

다음 빈칸을 채워 부가의문문을 완성하세요.

1. You don't love me, (   ) (   )?

2. She likes you, (   ) (   )?

3. He is the most handsome boy in our class, (   ) (   )?

4. Tom will go to bed soon, (   ) (   )?

5. We should do our best, (   ) (   )?

6. This movie is really funny, (   ) (   )?

7. You have a boy friend, (   ) (   )?

8. You can swim well, (   ) (   )?

9. The office closes on the weekend, (   ) (   )?

10. We don't have to wear these clothes, (   ) (   )?

---- **Exercise 1-1** --

다음 빈칸을 채워 부가의문문을 완성하세요.

1. She is pretty, (   ) (   )?

2. They are so kind, (   ) (   )?

3. We have to eat lunch, (   ) (   )?

4. I have good friends, (   ) (   )?

5. He studies hard, (   ) (   )?

6. We are going to see the movie, (   ) (   )?

7. You don't have enough money, (   ) (   )?

8. She doesn't hate me, (   ) (   )?

9. They can drive a truck, (   ) (   )?

10. She has to do it now, (   ) (   )?

Unit 21 감탄문

- what + a + 형용사 + 명사(+주어+동사)!
- how + 형용사/부사 (+주어+동사)!

Gorilla Grammar

unit 21 감탄문

1 what + a + 형용사 + 명사 (+ 주어 + 동사)!

- What a kind boy (he is)!

  그는 정말 친절한 소년이구나!

- What a nice house (it is)!

  그것은 정말 멋진 집이다!

- What beautiful eyes (you have)!

  너는 정말 아름다운 눈을 가지고 있구나!

2 how + 형용사/부사 (+ 주어 + 동사)!

- How brave (you are)!

  너는 정말 용감하구나!

- How useful (the machine is)!

  이 기계는 정말 유용하구나!

---- **Exercise 1** ---

다음 문장의 틀린 부분을 옳게 고치세요.

1. What nice car it is!

→

2. How the flower is beautiful!

→

3. What kind the teacher is!

→

4. How a delicious cake it is!

→

5. What a handsome man are you!

→

6. How kind is the girl!

→

7. What a funny movie is!

→

8. What interesting novels are they!

→

9. How boring this book it is!

→

10. What a tall boy it is!

→

---- **Exercise 1-1** --

다음 문장의 틀린 부분을 옳게 고치세요.

1. What a delicious apple is it!

→

2. How a nice car it is!

→

3. What a beautiful picture is!

→

4. How gorgeous is the room!

→

5. What a boring book they are!

→

6. What a funny drama is it!

→

7. How gentle the man he is!

→

8. How beautiful the house it is!

→

9. What a nice car they are!

→

10. How a great pen it is!

→

Unit 19 비교급 및 최상급   Unit 20 부가의문문   Unit 21 감탄문

1 다음 빈칸에 들어갈 말로 알맞지 <u>않은</u> 것은?

> Her story is_____than yours.

① funny
② better
③ shorter
④ much longer
⑤ more interesting

2 다음 빈칸에 들어갈 말이 바르게 짝지어진 것은?

> • Kevin is even _____than Ted.
> • Kevin is the_____boy in the team.

① strong-stronger
② stronger-strongest
③ strong-strongest
④ strongest-strong
⑤ stronger-stronger

3 비교급과 최상급의 형태가 바르게 짝지어진 것은?

① early - earlyer -earlyest
② long - longger - longgest
③ well - better - best
④ bad - badder- baddest
⑤ famous - famouser-famousest

4 빈칸에 들어갈 가장 알맞은 말을 고르세요.

> Her story is_____than yours.

① well
② worse
③ bad
④ good
⑤ best

5 다음 대화의 빈칸에 알맞은 것은?

> A: How are you today?
> B: I feel_____than yesterday.

① good
② well
③ nice
④ better
⑤ best

6 다음 주어진 문장과 뜻이 일치하는 것은?

> No river is as long as the Nile.

① The Nile is not a long river.
② No river is as short as the Nile.
③ The Nile is the longest river.
④ Many rivers are longer than the Nile.
⑤ The Nile is not so long as the river.

7 다음 두 문장을 한 문장으로 고칠 때 빈칸에 들어갈 말로 알맞은 것은?

> • Jack received an A in math. Mary received a B in math.
> • Jack did _____ in math than Mary.

① well
② better
③ bad
④ good
⑤ best

8 다음 중 어법상 바른 문장은?

① Susan is as taller as Peter.
② It's fastest animal in the world.
③ You look happyer than yesterday.
④ Seoul is one of the oldest city in the world.
⑤ Please speak more slowly.

9 다음 빈칸에 들어갈 말이 바르게 짝지어진 것은?

> • _____ a brave boy he is!
> • _____ cute your dog is!

① What - What
② How - Why
③ What - How
④ Why - What
⑤ How - How

10 다음 우리말과 일치하도록 주어진 단어를 배열하세요.

> 그 고양이는 지저분해, 그렇지 않니?
> (it / the cat / , / is / dirty / isn't)

→ _____?

11 다음 중 밑줄 친 부분이 어법상 틀린 것은?

① You will meet her, <u>won't</u> you?
② They play the piano well, <u>don't they</u>?
③ Your sister can ride a bicycle, <u>can't she</u>?
④ He reads a newspaper every morning, <u>don't he</u>?
⑤ She didn't finish her homework, <u>did she</u>?

12 다음 밑줄 친 부분과 바꿔 쓸수 있는 것은?

> Your mother plays the violin well, <u>right</u>?

① can't she
② doesn't she
③ does she
④ isn't it
⑤ is she

13 다음 문장을 감탄문으로 고친 것 중 <u>틀린</u> 것은?

① He is very nice.
　 How nice he is!
② She is very kind.
　 How kind she is!
③ It is a very pretty bag.
　 What a pretty bag is it!
④ We are very good friends.
　 What good friends we are!
⑤ It is very interesting news.
　 What interesting news it is!

14 다음 주어진 문장과 의미가 같은 것은? (2개)

> He has very cute dogs.

① How cute his dogs are!
② how cute dogs he has!
③ What cute his dogs are!
④ What very cute dogs he has!
⑤ What cute dogs he has!

15 다음 대화의 빈칸에 알맞은 것은?

> A: Marina is good at English,_____?
> B: Yes, she is.

① does she
② don't she
③ is she
④ isn't she
⑤ doesn't she

16 다음 빈칸에 들어갈 말이 순서대로 짝지어진 것은?

> • _____great this movie is!
> • _____hot water this is!
> • _____smart that boy is!

① How - How - How
② How - What - What
③ How - What - How
④ What -What - What
⑤ What - What - How

17 다음 우리말에 맞도록 빈칸에 알맞은 말을 쓰세요.

> 너는 거짓말을 안 할 거지, 그렇지?
> You won't tell any lies, _____?

[18-20] 주어진 단어를 알맞은 형태로 고쳐 빈칸에 쓰세요.

18 Suji is_____than Sora. (pretty)

19 Baseball is_____than soccer in Cuba. (popular)

20 This elephant is_____animal in this zoo. (big)

21 다음 우리말과 일치하도록 빈칸에 알맞은 말을 쓰세요.

정말 큰 비행기구나!

→ _____ _____ _____airplane!

22 다음 문장을 How로 시작하는 감탄문으로 고쳐 쓰세요.

The doll is very pretty.

→ _____

23 다음 중 밑줄 친 부분이 어법상 틀린 것은?

① He reads a newspaper, <u>isn't he</u>?
② You will see a doctor, <u>won't you</u>?
③ Tim plays the guitar well, <u>doesn't he</u>?
④ Your brother can drive a car, <u>can't he</u>?
⑤ She didn't finish her homework, <u>did she</u>?

주니어 고릴라 영문법
Junior Gorilla Grammar

주니어

고릴라
영문법

Junior Gorilla Grammar

Level 1

| 정답 및 해설 |

Unit 1 단어의 종류
본문 p.5

Exercise 1) 다음 제시된 단어의 종류를 하나만 작성하세요.

1. 명사 / 2. 동사 / 3. 형용사 / 4. 형용사 / 5. 부사 /
6. 명사 / 7. 부사 / 8. 명사 / 9. 명사 / 10. 동사

Exercise 1-1) 다음 제시된 단어의 종류를 하나만 작성하세요.

1. 형용사 / 2. 부사 / 3. 동사 / 4. 명사 / 5. 동사 / 6.
형용사 / 7. 부사 / 8. 명사, 동사 / 9. 명사 / 10. 동사

Unit 2 인칭대명사

Exercise 1) 다음 해석에 맞게 빈칸을 채우세요.
본문 p.8

1. They / 2. She / 3. You / 4. We / 5. He /
6. I / 7. They / 8. It / 9. She / 10. He

Exercise 1-1) 다음 해석에 맞게 빈칸을 채우세요.

1. It / 2. You / 3. She / 4. It / 5. She / 6. He /
7. They / 8. They / 9. I / 10. We

Exercise 2) 다음 해석에 맞게 빈칸을 채우세요.
본문 p.10

1. you / 2. him / 3. it / 4. me / 5. them / 6. me /
7. you / 8. her / 9. you / 10. us

Exercise 3) 다음 해석에 맞게 빈칸을 채우세요.

1. my / 2. your / 3. his / 4. their / 5. your /
6. my / 7. Our / 8. our / 9. Their / 10. My

Exercise 3-1) 다음 해석에 맞게 빈칸을 채우세요.
본문 p.12

1. my / 2. her / 3. your / 4. Our / 5. my / 6. our
/ 7. his / 8. her / 9. your / 10. Their

Exercise 4) 다음 해석에 맞게 빈칸을 채우세요.

1. I / 2. me / 3. his / 4. They / 5. you / 6. him /
7. He / 8. Her / 9. us / 10. them

Exercise 5) 다음 문장의 밑줄 친 부분을 바르게 고쳐 쓰세요.
본문 p.14

1. mine / 2. ours / 3. hers / 4. his / 5. theirs /
6. mine / 7. yours / 8. ours / 9. hers / 10. mine

Exercise 5-1) 다음 문장의 밑줄 친 부분을 바르게 고쳐 쓰세요.

1. yours / 2. ours / 3. hers / 4. yours / 5. theirs
/ 6. mine / 7. his / 8. hers / 9. ours / 10. mine

Unit 3 명령문
본문 p.18

Exercise 1) 다음 문장을 명령문으로 바꾸세요.

1. Be kind to everyone.
2. Don't open the door.
3. Close the window.
4. Come here.
5. Be quiet.

Exercise 1-1) 다음 문장을 명령문으로 바꾸세요.

1. Do your homework right now.
2. Never tell a lie.
3. Be generous with your time.
4. Don't say that again.
5. Don't be lazy.

Exercise 2) 다음 문장을 영작하세요.
본문 p.19

1. Don't say goodbye.
2. Be happy.
3. Never call me again. (Don't call me again.)
4. Come here.
5. Sleep soundly.

Exercise 2-1) 다음 문장을 영작하세요.

1. Don't worry.
2. Don't ride the bicycle without a helmet.
3. Look at me.
4. Clean your room right now.
5. Don't be angry.

■ 단원별 문제

| unit 1 단어의 종류
| unit 2 인칭대명사
| unit 3 명령문

본문 p.20

1. ③
tip! ①은 명사, ②는 부사, ④는 형용사, ⑤는 동사이다.
2. ③
tip! Them은 They로 바뀌어야 한다.
3. ⑤
tip! 나머지는 다 주격과 목적격의 관계인데 ⑤번만 주격 (또는 목적격)과 소유격의 관계이다.
4. ③
tip! 명사를 꾸며주는 것은 형용사로, soft가 이에 해당된다.
5. ①
tip! their → them 으로 바뀌어야 한다.
6. ②
tip! 빈 칸은 동사가 들어갈 자리로, be late 으로 바뀌어야 빈 칸에 들어 갈 수 있다.
7. ②
tip! my → me로 바꾸면 4형식 문장이 되어 '그녀는 나에게 비밀을 얘기해주었다.'로 해석이 된다.
8. ③
9. He
10. ③
tip!
A: Is this his book? (이거 그의 책이니?)
B: Yes, it's   his . (응, 이것은 그의 것이야.)
11. ④
12. ①, ④
13. ③
14. don't/ do not
15. ②
16. closes → close
tip! 명령문은 동사원형으로 시작한다.
17. They
18. H(h)er
19. (1) her (2) They
20. 6개 tip! yesterday, Sure, also, really, so 2개

Unit 4 be 동사

(1) 동사의 종류
(2) be동사의 축약형

본문 p.26

Exercise 1) 다음 문장의 빈칸에 am, are, is 중 알맞은 것을 쓰세요.
1. are / 2. is / 3. am / 4. are / 5. are / 6. are / 7. are / 8. Am / 9. is / 10. is

Exercise 1-1) 다음 문장의 빈칸에 am, are, is 중 알맞은 것을 쓰세요.
1. is / 2. is / 3. is / 4. are / 5. is / 6. are / 7. am / 8. is / 9. are / 10. is

본문 p.28

Exercise 2) 다음 문장의 빈칸에 was, were 중 알맞은 것을 쓰세요.
1. was / 2. were / 3. was / 4. was / 5. was / 6. were / 7. was / 8. were / 9. was / 10. was

Exercise 2-1) 다음 문장의 빈칸에 was, were 중 알맞은 것을 쓰세요.
1. were / 2. was / 3. was / 4. was / 5. were / 6. were / 7. were / 8. was / 9. were / 10. was

본문 p.30

Exercise 3) 다음 문장의 밑줄 친 부분을 줄여서 다시 쓰세요.
1. You're 6 years old.
2. He's happy.
3. They're so kind.
4. I'm your friend.
5. She's a doctor.
6. We're in your house.
7. It's sunny.
8. That's not your fault.

Exercise 3-1) 다음 문장의 밑줄 친 부분을 줄여서 다시 쓰세요.
1. It's time to leave.
2. That's a good idea.

3. I'm a middle school student.

4. He's such a gentleman.

5. She's so lovely.

6. We're good at English.

7. You're gorgeous.

8. They're not idiots.

(3) be동사의 부정문

본문 p.33

Exercise 1) 다음 문장의 밑줄 친 부분을 줄여서 다시 쓰세요.

1. He's not my uncle.

2. She isn't my daughter.

3. They're not my friends.

4. We're not students.

5. You aren't bad.

6. I'm not that kind of a man.

7. We're not happy.

8. You aren't fat.

9. These aren't mine.

10. She's not my girl friend.

본문 p.34

Exercise 1-1) 다음 문장의 밑줄 친 부분을 줄여서 다시 쓰세요.

1. She isn't my cousin.

2. He's not my son.

3. They're not students.

4. This isn't your money.

5. She's not a girl any more.

6. He's not gentle.

7. We aren't sad.

8. I'm not crazy.

9. He's not rich.

10. You aren't hungry.

Exercise 2) 다음 문장을 부정문으로 바꾸어 쓰세요.

1. The boy was not very friendly.

2. We are not happy.

3. I am not a boy.

4. She is not so kind.

5. He was not rich.

6. This book is not mine.

7. Those were not enough for me.

8. The chair is not comfortable.

9. I was not a painter.

10. They are not from Korea.

본문 p.36

Exercise 2-1) 다음 문장을 부정문으로 바꾸어 쓰세요.

1. We are not good friends.

2. They were not from Japan.

3. He is not a famous singer.

4. You are not tall.

5. He was not handsome.

6. She is not having dinner now.

7. We were not going to go to school.

8. They are not so friendly.

9. I was not fine.

10. That is not enough.

(4) be동사의 의문문

본문 p.38

Exercise 1) 다음 문장을 의문문으로 바꾸어 쓰세요.

1. Was I a student?

2. Is Tom generous?

3. Was she cute?

4. Were you my friend?

5. Is she beautiful?

6. Is her name Jane?

7. Was red my favorite color?

8. Are you happy?

9. Were you leaving?

10. Are they good at swimming?

Exercise 1-1) 다음 문장을 의문문으로 바꾸어 쓰세요.

1. Was John your roommate?

2. Is she lovely?

3. Was he from Brazil?

4. Is Tom hungry?

5. Were You alone?

6. Am I single?

7. Are we in the pool?

8. Were they so kind?

9. Is she smart?

10. Was he good at running?

본문 p.40

Exercise 2) 주어진 단어를 이용하여 영작하세요.

1. She is not pretty.

2. He is very handsome.

3. They are kind.

4. Are you alone?

5. I'm (at) home.

6. She was sick.

7. He is not Japanese.

8. Are you busy now?

9. It was very beautiful.

10. Time is gold.

Exercise 2-1) 주어진 단어를 이용하여 영작하세요.

1. Is she intelligent?

2. Is Tom diligent?

3. She isn't tall.

4. This baby is so cute.

5. She was my first love.

6. Is this watch yours?

7. He was a student last year.

8. They are very tall.

9. The movie was so fun.

10. You and I are the same age.

본문 p.42

Exercise 3) 다음 질문에 긍정과 부정으로 대답하세요.

1. 긍정 → Yes, she is. / 부정 → No. she isn't.

2. 긍정 → Yes, I am. / 부정 → No, I'm not.

3. 긍정 → Yes, I am. / 부정 → No, I'm not.

4. 긍정 → Yes, they are. / 부정 → No, they aren't.

5. 긍정 → Yes, he is. / 부정 → No, he isn't.

6. 긍정 → Yes, he was. / 부정 → No, he wasn't.

7. 긍정 → Yes, they were. / 부정 → No, they weren't.

8. 긍정 → Yes, there was. / 부정 → No, there wasn't.

9. 긍정 → Yes, he was. / 부정 → No he wasn't.

10. 긍정 → Yes, it was. / 부정 → No, it wasn't.

본문 p.44

Exercise 3-1) 다음 질문에 긍정과 부정으로 대답하세요.

1. 긍정 → Yes, he(she) is. / 부정 → No, he(she) isn't.

2. 긍정 → Yes, we are. / 부정 → No, we aren't.

3. 긍정 → Yes, I am. / 부정 → No, I'm not.

4. 긍정 → Yes, she is. / 부정 → No, she isn't.

5. 긍정 → Yes, they are. / 부정 → No, they aren't.

6. 긍정 → Yes, he was. / 부정 → No, he wasn't.

7. 긍정 → Yes, she was. / 부정 → No, she wasn't.

8. 긍정 → Yes, I was. / 부정 → No, I wasn't.

9. 긍정 → Yes, he was. / 부정 → No, he wasn't.

10. 긍정 → Yes, they were. / 부정 → No, they weren't.

Unit 5 일반 동사

(1) 일반 동사의 3인칭 단수 현재형 만들기
본문 p.48

Exercise 1) 다음 밑줄 친 부분을 옳게 고치세요.

1. He eats bread for lunch.

2. She wants to go out.

3. He goes to bed early.

4. We have a lot of books.

5. He works hard.

6. Tom teaches them English.

7. She always sleeps well.

8. He enjoys reading.

9. Time flies!

10. Jane solves problems.

Exercise 1-1) 다음 밑줄 친 부분을 옳게 고치세요.

1. Jane always helps people in need.

2. I watch TV.

3. It sounds great!

4. They go to the movies.

5. He sometimes lends me money.

6. He fixes it by himself.

7. She always waits for them.

8. That picture looks great!
9. She meets Korean friends regularly.
10. He hopes that he can solve the problem.

(2) 일반 동사의 과거형 만들기 (규칙)

본문 p.51

Exercise 1) 다음 주어진 단어들의 과거형을 쓰세요.
1. robbed / 2. agreed / 3. married / 4. hoped /
5. loved / 6. changed / 7. studied / 8. hated / 9.
dropped / 10. admitted / 11. occurred /
12. fried / 13. played / 14. turned

Exercise 1-1) 다음 주어진 단어들의 과거형을 쓰세요.
1. stopped / 2. climbed / 3. begged / 4. talked /
5. closed / 6. carried / 7. cleaned / 8. planned /
9. hurried / 10. offered / 11. called / 12. died /
13. enjoyed / 14. ended

본문 p.52

Exercise 2) 다음 문장을 과거형 문장으로 변환하세요.
1. Traffic accidents occurred very often.
2. I talked to you.
3. They called me John.
4. We played soccer together.
5. The store opened at 7a.m.

Exercise 3) 다음 문장을 영작하세요. (규칙동사)
1. He stayed there for quite a long time.
2. They played computer games yesterday.
3. I visited Seoul with my friends.
4. Tom died 3 years ago.
5. I studied English hard this morning.

Exercise 3-1) 다음 문장을 영작하세요. (규칙동사)
1 She carried the books in the bag.
2. He entered my house again.
3. I married her 2 days ago.
4. He dried his hair with a fan.
5. She changed her e-mail address yesterday.

(3) 일반 동사의 과거형 만들기 (불규칙)

본문 p.55

Exercise 1) 다음 주어진 단어들의 과거형을 쓰세요.
1. was, were / 2. found / 3. came / 4. gave /
5. grew / 6. became / 7. heard / 8. got / 9. did
/ 10. built / 11. went / 12. bought / 13. hurt /
14. felt

Exercise 1-1) 다음 주어진 단어들의 과거형을 쓰세요.
1. made / 2. sent / 3. met / 4. told / 5. put /
6. knew / 7. ran / 8. read / 9. taught / 10. said /
11. took / 12. sold / 13. saw / 14. thought

본문 p.56

Exercise 2) 다음 문장을 과거형 문장으로 변환하세요.
(불규칙 동사)
1. I made myself understood.
2. She slept less than 5 hours.
3. I taught her how to cook.
4. They gave me a bouquet of flowers.
5. They kept the secret.
6. The wind began to blow.
7. I hid the comic book under the bed.
8. My brother drove the bus.
9. We sang a song together.
10. I drank alcohol almost everyday.

Exercise 2-1) 다음 문장을 과거형 문장으로 변환하세요.
(혼합형)
1. I wanted to play basketball.
2. She moved toward the window.
3. We won the game without your help.
4. I saw her in the hospital.
5. He felt nervous before a test.
6. I stayed at home on Sunday.
7. She entered the room.
8. I passed the exam.
9. I was not a stranger.
10. She called me several times.

Exercise 3) 다음 주어진 단어를 적절히 변형하여영작
하세요.(불규칙동사)
본문 p.58

1. Tom brought her to the hospital.
2. She hit me yesterday.
3. She gave me a candy.
4. Jane left without saying goodbye.
5. I told him something wrong.
6. Mr. Lee read a book last Sunday.
7. He cut paper with a knife.
8. I took an English test yesterday.
9. They built the bridge 3 years ago.
10. He knew her well.

Exercise 3-1) 다음 주어진 단어를 적절히 변형하여
영작하세요. (혼합형)

1. He understood everything about me.
2. People lost their houses.
3. I liked everything about you.
4. She read the book yesterday.
5. We ate pizza for lunch.
6. I chose Jane instead of Sally.
7. I took a shower before going to bed yesterday.
8. I thought that he was talkative.
9. He found the watch.
10. The class ended in 10 minutes.

(4) 일반 동사의 의문문 만들기

Exercise 1) 다음 현재시제로 쓴 문장을 의문문으로
변환하세요.
본문 p.61

1. Does he dry his hair with this towel?
2. Does she run fast?
3. Do they go to church every Sunday?
4. Do I need a doctor?
5. Do we want to solve the problem?
6. Does Tom eat a lot?
7. Does he give me some money?
8. Do I know her well?

9. Does she enjoy watching the movie?
10. Does he miss her so much?

Exercise 1-1) 다음 과거시제로 쓴 문장을 의문문으로
변환하세요.
본문 p.62

1. Did she go to the movies?
2. Did he sleep well?
3. Did you open the door?
4. Did they remember you?
5. Did the plane arrive on time?
6. Did she love me?
7. Did he enjoy singing?
8. Did she watch the play?
9. Did they lend me the chair?
10. Did the lion push the bus?

Exercise 1-2) 다음 문장을 의문문으로 변환하세요.

1. Did he borrow this car for a week?
2. Does she ride a horse?
3. Did Tom like you?
4. Do I love you?
5. Do they go to church?
6. Did we make this cake for him?
7. Does she listen to music?
8. Did I buy a pair of shoes?
9. Do we need your help?
10. Does she leave on time?

Exercise 1-3) 다음 문장을 의문문으로 변환하세요.
본문 p.64

1. Does he solve mysteries?
2. Do we ride bicycles together?
3. Did the gorilla learn to speak?
4. Did my dad give me a present?
5. Did you finish your homework?
6. Did he meet her last Sunday?
7. Did they help me a lot?
8. Do we eat meat for dinner?
9. Does he come home early?
10. Did they love us?

Exercise 2) 다음 질문에 알맞은 대답을 쓰세요.
1. 긍정 → Yes, I do. / 부정 → No, I don't.
2. 긍정 → Yes, he did. / 부정 → No, he didn't.
3. 긍정 → Yes, I do. / 부정 → No, I don't.
4. 긍정 → Yes, I did. / 부정 → No, I didn't.
5. 긍정 → Yes, you do. / 부정 → No, you don't.

본문 p.66
Exercise 2-1) 다음 질문에 알맞은 대답을 쓰세요.
1. 긍정 → Yes, they did. / 부정 → No, they didn't.
2. 긍정 → Yes, he(she) did. / 부정 → No, he(she) didn't.
3. 긍정 → Yes, she did. / 부정 → No, she didn't.
4. 긍정 → Yes, they do. / 부정 → No, they don't.
5. 긍정 → Yes, he does. / 부정 → No, he doesn't.

(5) 일반 동사의 부정문 만들기
본문 p.68
Exercise 1) 다음 주어진 문장을 부정문으로 바꾸세요.
1. I don't miss her.
2. The store doesn't open at 10 a.m.
3. They didn't fight for liberty.
4. She didn't talk to him.
5. She doesn't live in Busan.
6. You didn't buy the car.
7. She didn't play the violin.
8. He doesn't drive a car.
9. They don't know each other.
10. I didn't do it.

Exercise 1-1) 다음 주어진 문장을 부정문으로 바꾸세요.
1. I didn't do something wrong.
2. She doesn't do something wrong.
3. They don't do something wrong.
4. She didn't take a bus.
5. They don't have dinner.
6. We don't do it well.
7. I didn't ask him a favor.
8. She doesn't often lend him some books.
9. We didn't bring the umbrellas.
10. He doesn't sleep deeply.

■ 단원별 문제
| unit 4 be 동사
| unit 5 일반동사

본문 p.70

1. ②
tip! Kate는 3인칭 단수이므로 is가 와야 한다.
2. ②
tip! This is는 축약형을 사용하지 않는다.
3. We are not late.
4. He was not a painter.
5. ④
① I am a singer. (o)
② My uncle, Sam is an engineer. (o)
③ Mary and Jennifer are in the library.
(o)
⑤ His books are on the desk. (o)
6. ②
7. ③
8. ③
tip! 동사를 is를 쓰기 위해서는 주어가 3인칭 단수여야 한다.
9. (1) He walks to school.
   (2) She watches basketball on TV every
       weekend.
   (3) I always don't bring my textbooks.
   (4) They have three dogs.
10. ①
11. She plays the piano in the school band.
12. ②
tip! he는 3인칭 단수형이기 때문에 현재형일 때
동사에 s를 붙여줘야 한다.
13. ②
14. ②
15. ③
tip! Does에 이미 -s가 표현되었기 때문에 주어 뒤
에 나오는 동사는 원형이 나와야한다.
16. ③
17. ③
tip! Does your dad always busy? → Is your
dad always busy?

18. ①
tip! She doesn't always has breakfast.
 → She doesn't always have breakfast.
19. ③
20. A: Were B: was

Unit 6 현재진행형

(1) 동사의 ing형 만들기

본문 p.76

Exercise 1) 다음 주어진 동사들의 +ing형을 쓰세요.
1. reading / 2. hitting / 3. lying / 4. doing /
5. stopping / 6. studying / 7. admitting /
8. teaching / 9. going / 10. having / 11. buying
/ 12. saying / 13. making / 14. feeling

Exercise 1-1) 다음 주어진 동사들의 +ing형을 쓰세요.
1. selling / 2. lying / 3. running / 4. finding /
5. dying / 6. cutting / 7. taking / 8. seeing /
9. knowing / 10. saying / 11. growing /
12. being / 13. building / 14 doing

Exercise 2) 다음 주어진 문장을 현재진행형 문장으로 바꿔 쓰세요.
1. Mom is washing the dishes.
2. I am sleeping in the room.
3. He is playing the computer game.
4. Jane is having dinner.
5. He is coming home late.
6. Dad is walking fast.
7. I am taking the bus.
8. They are riding horses.
9. She is playing the guitar.
10. You are wearing a pretty dress.

본문 p.78

Exercise 2-1) 다음 주어진 문장을 현재진행형 문장으로 바꿔 쓰세요.
1. I am catching the ball.
2. They are eating pizza.
3. I am using this pen.
4. We are opening the door.
5. You are studying hard.
6. He is running away from them.
7. We are crying loudly.
8. She is taking a picture.
9. He is passing the line.
10. The horse is running fast.

(2) 현재진행형의 의문문과 부정문 및 대답하기

본문 p.79

Exercise 1) 다음 문장을 의문문과 부정문으로 바꾸세요.
1. Is she watching the accident? / She isn't watching the accident.
2. Am I eating chicken now? / I am not eating chicken now.
3. Is he doing his homework? / He is not doing his homework.
4. Is she wearing new shoes? / She is not wearing new shoes.
5. Are they writing a letter? / They are not writing a letter.
6. Am I having lunch now? / I am not having lunch now.
7. Is he cleaning the windows? / He is not cleaning the windows.
8. Are we playing the piano? / We are not playing the piano.
9. Is she singing a song? / She is not singing a song.
10. Is he drawing a picture? / He is not drawing a picture.

Exercise 1-1) 다음 문장을 의문문과 부정문으로 바꾸세요.
1. Am I reading a book? / I am not reading a book.
2. Is the girl driving a car? / The girl is not driving a car.

3. Are they fishing illegally? / They are not fishing illegally.

4. Are we going to the gym? / We are not going to the gym.

5. Is he running toward her? / He is not running toward her.

6. Is she sleeping? / She is not sleeping.

7. Are they shouting loudly? / They aren't shouting loudly.

8. Is the bird flying high? / The bird is not flying high.

9. Are we lifting stones? / We are not lifting stones.

10. Am I putting the presents into the box? / I'm not putting the presents into the box.

본문 p.83

Exercise 2) 다음 문장에 긍정과 부정으로 대답하세요.

1. 긍정 → Yes, I am. / 부정 → No, I'm not.
2. 긍정 → Yes, I am. / 부정 → No, I'm not.
3. 긍정 → Yes, she is. / 부정 → No, she isn't.
4. 긍정 → Yes, he is. / 부정 → No, he isn't.
5. 긍정 → Yes, we are. / 부정 → No, we aren't.
6. 긍정 → Yes, they are. / 부정 → No, they aren't.
7. 긍정 → Yes, he is. / 부정 → No, he isn't.
8. 긍정 → Yes, he is. / 부정 → No, he isn't.
9. 긍정 → Yes, she is. / 부정 → No, she isn't.
10. 긍정 → Yes, I am. / 부정 → No, I'm not.

(3) 현재와 현재진행형의 비교
본문 p.86

Exercise 1) 다음 중 올바른 표현을 고르세요.

1. play / 2. is watching / 3. are jogging / 4. rains / 5. is falling / 6. usually reads / 7. falls / 8. is playing / 9. belongs / 10. know

Exercise 1-1) 다음 중 올바른 표현을 고르세요.

1. hate / 2. is taking / 3. is boiling / 4. do you do / 5. go / 6. boils / 7. am listening / 8. is talking / 9. am swimming / 10. speak

본문 p.88

Exercise 2) 다음 주어진 문장을 현재진행형 문장으로 영작하세요.

1. I am not playing the piano.
2. She is waiting for you.
3. I am talking on the phone with Tom.
4. They are playing soccer.
5. She is not swimming.
6. I am walking in the rain.
7. You are not speaking loudly.
8. She is smiling at the child.
9. Mr. Kim is fishing.
10. She is not studying hard.

Exercise 3) 다음 주어진 문장을 적절한 시제를 사용하여 영작하세요.

1. Water is boiling.
2. I go to church every Sunday.
3. She works at the office.
4. I am not sleeping.
5. I go to bed before midnight.
6. She is not having dinner.
7. Tom has three dogs.
8. She has brown eyes.
9. The store opens at 7 a.m.
10. The boy is not taking a shower.

본문 p.90

Exercise 3-1) 다음 주어진 문장을 적절한 시제를 사용하여 영작하세요.

1. He is honest.
2. She is running toward him now.
3. She doesn't have the bag.
4. They are playing basketball.
5. I didn't tell him the story.
6. I watch a movie every Sunday.
7. I am watching the movie.
8. He didn't go to church yesterday.
9. A rabbit has long ears.
10. The dog is barking now.

Unit 7 미래를 나타내는 will과 be going to

(1) will과 be going to의 비교
본문 p.93

Exercise 1) 다음 주어진 문장에서 <u>틀린 부분</u>을 찾아서 고치세요.

1. goes → go
2. meeting → meet
3. passes → pass
4. call → to call
5. being → be
6. go → going
7. cleaned → clean
8. telling → tell
9. graduating → graduate
10. to marry → marry

Exercise 2) 다음 주어진 문장을 영작하세요.
본문 p.94

1. I'm going to go to Japan this summer.
2. I will clean my room.
3. I will become a doctor.
4. Dad is going to cook lunch for us.
5. I will tell her about the accident tonight.

Exercise 2-1) 다음 주어진 문장을 영작하세요.

1. His dream will come true someday.
2. I am going to visit him next year.
3. I am going to go swimming tomorrow.
4. One day, she will be back.
5. Too much anger will kill you.

(2) 부정문과 의문문 만들기
본문 p.96

Exercise 1) 다음 주어진 문장을 의문문과 부정문으로 고치세요.

1. Will she be ok? / She will not be ok.
2. Will he come back? / He won't come back.
3. Will she drive me crazy? / She won't drive me crazy.

4. Am I going to see you soon? / I am not going to see you soon.
5. Will we visit America? / We won't visit America.

Exercise 1-1) 다음 주어진 문장을 의문문과 부정문으로 고치세요.

1. Will it rain tomorrow? / It will not rain tomorrow.
2. Will he call us? / He will not call us.
3. Are you going to go home? / You are not going to go home.
4. Are they going to have dinner? / They aren't going to have dinner.
5. Will I pass the exam? / I will not pass the exam.

Exercise 2) 다음 주어진 문장을 영작하세요.
본문 p.98

1. Will you close the window?
2. It will be very boring.
3. We are not going to dance together.
4. I am going to go to bed late today.
5. Will he become a teacher?

Exercise 2-1) 다음 주어진 문장을 영작하세요.

1. Are you going to go to church this Sunday?
2. He is going to order the food.
3. I will live in the USA someday.
4. Are you going to give him some chocolate?
5. She will not swim in the river this summer.

■ 단원별 문제
| unit 6 현재진행형
| unit 7 미래를 나타내는 will과 be going to
본문 p.100

1. ⑤
tip! waitting → waiting
2. ⑤
3. ①
4. ②
5. Are you reading a newspaper?
6. ⑤
tip! Sure (물론이지)라고 대답했으니 긍정문으로 표현해야 한다. 따라서 Sure, I will go. 가 옳은 표현이다.
7. ①
8. ③
9. ④
tip! ④의 is going to는 미래표현이기 때문에 yesterday랑 어울리지 않는다.
10. ②
11. ②
tip! 조동사 다음에는 동사의 원형이 와야 하며, 이는 부정문일 때도 적용된다.
12. ①
13. ①
tip! 미래를 나타내는 표현인 be going to 다음에 동사원형이 온다.
14. ④
tip! will과 be going to는 의미가 유사하다.
15. ③
tip! will은 미래를 나타내는 조동사이다.
16. (1) taking (2) studying
17. ③
18. ③
tip! she와 are은 어울리지 않다.
19. ④
tip! ④ I don't → I am not (혹은 I'm not)
20. (1) am, doing (2) Are, working (3) is, sitting

Unit 8 비인칭 주어 it

본문 p.105

Exercise 1) 대명사 It을 써서 다음 문장을 영작하세요.
1. It is fine today.
2. It is winter now.
3. What time is it now?
4. It is eleven thirty.
5. What day is it today?
6. It is Friday.
7. It is raining.
8. It was cold yesterday.
9. How far is it?
10. It's about 5km.

Exercise 1-1) 대명사 It을 써서 다음 문장을 영작하세요.
1. It is Wednesday today.
2. It is 5p.m. now.
3. It is very easy.
4. It is so hot today.
5. It is winter now.
6. What time is it?
7. It is true.
8. It was me.
9. It was very hot yesterday.
10. It is raining outside now.

Unit 9 There is /There are

본문 p.109

Exercise 1) 다음 문장에서 문법적으로 틀린 부분을 찾아 고치세요.

1. There is a car
2. There is a book.
3. There are many people.
4. There were your cars.
5. There is some money in his pocket.
6. There is a table.
7. There were three cats.
8. There are many pens.
9. There is a notebook.
10. There were two birds and one dog.

본문 p.110

Exercise 2) 다음 문장을 지시하는 대로 바꾸세요.

1. Is there a book on the table?
   There isn't a book on the table.
2. Are there three apples?
   There are not three apples.
3. Is there only one bed in my room?
   There isn't only one bed in my room.
4. Are there many people?
   There are not many people.
5. Was there a new watch under the chair?
   There was not a new watch under the chair.
6. Were there a lot of pens in the pencil case?
   There were not a lot of pens in the pencil case.
7. Is there much money in the envelope?
   There isn't much money in the envelope?
8. Are there my daughters?
   There are not my daughters.
9. Are there many cars?
   There aren't many cars.
10. Is there a new watch?
    There is not a new watch.

■ 단원별 문제

| unit 8 비인칭 주어 it
| unit 9 There is/ There are

1. ②
tip! ②에서의 it은 a book을 가리키는 지시대명사로 사용되었지만 나머지는 비인칭 주어로 사용됐다.
2. ②
tip! are → is
3. ④
tip! 보기의 it은 비인칭 주어로 쓴 it이다.
4. ②
tip! is → are
5. It
6. ④
7. There is an orange
8. ①
9. ①
tip! ①은 is가 적절하고 나머지는 are이 적절하다.
10. ②
11. it
12. ①
13. There is the answer.
14. There is a car on the street.
15. There is your umbrella in the corner.
16. There are my favorite games.
17. There is your lunch on the table.

Unit 10 조동사 can, may

(1) 조동사 기본 사항

본문 p.116

Exercise 1) 다음 문장에서 문법적으로 틀린 부분을 고치세요.

1. play → play
2. coming → come
3. will 이나 may → 삭제
4. going → go
5. am → be

Exercise 1-1) 다음 문장에서 문법적으로 틀린 부분을 고치세요.

1. does → do
2. cans → can
3. is → be
4. wrote → write
5. runs → run

(2) 허락과 허가의 조동사 can, may

본문 p.118

Exercise 1) 다음 질문에 적절한 대답을 쓰세요.

1. 긍정 → Yes, you may. / 부정 → No, you may not.
2. 긍정 → Yes, you can. / 부정 → No, you can't.
3. 긍정 → Yes, you can. / 부정 → No, you can't.
4. 긍정 → Yes, you may. / 부정 → No, you may not.
5. 긍정 → Yes, you may. / 부정 → No, you may not.

Exercise 2) 괄호 안의 단어를 참고하여 다음 문장을 영작하세요.

1. May I help you?
2. May I go home?
3. Can you lend me some money?
4. You can call me anytime.
5. May I use your pen?
6. May I leave a message?
7. You can call me John.
8. May I go to your house?
9. May I sit down on this chair?
10. You can park here.

(3) 가능의 조동사 can

본문 p.121

(4) 추측의 조동사 may

Exercise 1) 괄호 안의 단어를 참고하여 다음 문장을 영작하세요.

1. She can play the piano.
2. I cannot study any more.
3. He may be sleeping.
4. He may be a teacher.
5. I cannot eat any more.
6. The news may not be true.
7. My brother can speak Japanese.
8. The rumor may be true.

Unit 11 조동사 must, have to
본문 p.124

Exercise 1) 다음 주어진 문장을 주어진 단어를 활용하여 영작하세요. (긍정)

1. I have to leave now.
2. He must do his homework right now.
3. She must be living alone.
4. You have to come back home.
5. I must check my e-mail.

Exercise 1-1) 다음 주어진 문장을 주어진 단어를 활용하여 영작하세요. (긍정)

1. She must be poor.
2. I have to meet him today.
3. You must get up early tomorrow.
4. The dog must be hungry.
5. She has to stay home.

본문 p.125

Exercise 1-2) 다음 주어진 문장을 주어진 단어를 활용하여 영작하세요. (부정)

1. You don't have to do it now.
2. You must not buy the car.
3. You don't have to buy the car.
4. I must not yell at him.
5. He doesn't have to take a bus.

Exercise 1-3) 다음 주어진 문장을 주어진 단어를 활용하여 영작하세요. (혼합)

1. She must read this book.
2. He doesn't have to lend me money.
3. I have to play the piano.
4. I must not play the piano.
5. I don't have to play the piano.

■ **단원별 문제**

| unit 10 조동사 can, may
| unit 11 조동사 must, have to

본문 p.128

1. ②
tip! 허가를 나타내는 조동사에는 may와 can이 있다.

2. ⑤

3. ⑤
tip! 밑줄 친 Why not?은 '왜 안 되겠어?'라는 의미로 긍정의 대답이다.

4. ②
tip! 조동사를 포함한 문장을 부정문으로 만들 때는 조동사 바로 뒤에 부정어를 붙인다.

5. ②
tip! 조동사 바로 뒤에 동사원형이 온다.

6. ⑤
tip! must는 의무의 조동사이다. 따라서 해석은 '제가 당신께 질문을 해야만 하나요?'가 된다.

7. ②
tip! 한 문장에 조동사를 한 개 이상 사용하지 않는다.

8. ④
tip! 조동사 뒤에는 동사원형이 온다. 따라서 ④이 문법적으로 맞으려면 play가 되어야 한다.

9. ②

10. ①

11. ④
tip! have to는 수일치에 영향을 받는다. 주어가 My son이라는 3인칭 단수이므로 has to여야 한다.

12. ①
tip! ①의 may는 추측을 나타내고 나머지는 다 '~해도 좋다'라는 허가를 나타낸다.

13. ③

14. ①
tip! 보기에서 의무를 나타내는 조동사는 must밖에 없다.

15. ②
tip! 조동사를 포함한 문장을 부정문으로 만들 때는 조동사 뒤에 부정어를 붙이면 된다.

16. ②, ④

17. ⑤

18. Tom will do the dishes after dinner.
혹은 Tom does the dishes after dinner.
19. is able to
20. ②
tip! may 대신 쓸 수 있는 허가를 나타내는 조동사는 can이다.
21. ②
tip! ②번은 추측의 의미로 쓰여야지만 자연스럽다
22. ④
tip! You must not sleep here. (너는 여기서 자서는 안된다.)
You don't have to sleep here. (너는 여기서 잘 필요가 없다.)

Unit 12 감각동사
본문 p.132

Exercise 1) 다음 문장을 괄호 안의 감각동사를 활용하여 영작하세요.

1. She looks beautiful.
2. This food tastes delicious.
3. She felt happy.
4. Kimchi smells spicy.
5. That sounds great!
6. This bread smells bad.
7. The room looks clean.
8. This candle smells good.

Exercise 1-1) 다음 문장을 괄호 안의 감각동사를 활용하여 영작하세요.

1. The pie looks delicious.
2. The pizza smells good.
3. That sounds good.
4. I felt fresh.
5. She looks pretty.
6. You look like a model.
7. This smells like Japanese food.
8. This tastes like pizza.

Unit 13 4형식 동사
본문 p.137

Exercise 1) 다음 4형식 문장을 3형식 문장으로 바꾸세요.

1. She gave a book to me.
2. I tell the truth to him.
3. I bought a pair of earrings for her.
4. Jane wrote a letter to me.
5. I made a cake for you.
6. He sometimes lends some money to her.
7. He sent an e-mail to me.
8. They showed something funny to us.

Exercise 1-1) 다음 4형식은 3형식으로, 3형식은 4형식 문장으로 바꾸세요.

1. We can tell something special to you.
2. She gave some books to me.
3. He asked our vacation plan of her.
4. I can teach you English.
5. She showed her diary to me.
6. Mom made me a new dress.
7. She wrote us an e-mail.
8. I bought her a cell phone.

Unit 14 문장의 종류
본문 p.141

exercise 1) 다음 문장의 형식을 말하고 해석하세요.

1. 4형식 - 나의 엄마는 나에게 새 바지를 사주셨다.
2. 3형식 - 나의 엄마는 새 바지를 사셨다.
3. 2형식 - 그 우유는 상했다.
4. 3형식 - 나는 너와 결혼 할 것이다.
5. 2형식 - 나는 소년이다.
6. 3형식 - 나는 이 케익을 만들었다.
7. 2형식 - 그 계획은 재미있게 들린다.
8. 4형식 - 그녀는 나에게 반지 하나를 보여주었다.
9. 2형식 - 잎들이 녹색으로 변했다.
10. 5형식 - 그녀는 그를 변호사로 만들었다.

exercise 1-1) 다음 문장의 형식을 말하고 해석하세요. 본문 p.142

1. 5형식 - 그들은 나를 Bunny라고 부른다.
2. 1형식 - 그녀는 보통 늦게 잔다.
3. 3형식 - 나는 컴퓨터를 고쳤다.
4. 1형식 - 해는 동쪽에서 뜬다.
5. 2형식 - 그는 쉽게 잠들었다.
6. 5형식 - 우리는 그 소녀를 Jane이라고 이름 지었다.
7. 3형식 - 나는 매일 목욕한다.
8. 3형식 - 나는 어제 너의 가방을 원했다.
9. 4형식 - Jane은 그녀의 집 앞에서 나에게 돈을 좀 주었다.

exercise 1-2) 다음 문장의 형식을 말하고 해석하세요.

1. 2형식 - 나의 형은 키가 크다.
2. 1형식 - 책상위에 사과 하나가 있다.
3. 4형식 - 그는 나에게 종종 재미있는 얘기를 해준다.
4. 2형식 - 그는 잘 생겨 보인다.
5. 2형식 - 그 게임은 쉽지 않다.
6. 4형식 - 그들은 나에게 일주일에 두 번 영어를 가르친다.
7. 2형식 - 그녀는 의사가 되었다.
8. 1형식 - 나는 어제 심하게 울었다.
9. 1형식 - 그들은 방 안에 있다.

exercise 1-3) 다음 문장의 형식을 말하고 해석하세요. 본문 p.144

1. 1형식 - 나는 매일 달린다.
2. 5형식 - 우리는 바에서 그를 John이라고 불렀다.
3. 5형식 - 그는 나를 치과의사로 만들었다.
4. 3형식 - 나는 나의 모든 마음을 담아 편지를 썼다.
5. 3형식 - 나는 너를 위해 상자를 만든다.
6. 3형식 - 나는 그와 저녁을 먹었다.
7. 5형식 - 그녀는 나를 행복하게 만든다.
8. 2형식 - 너는 오늘 행복해 보이지 않는다.
9. 3형식 - 나는 가끔 피아노를 친다.
10. 2형식 - 너는 정말 예쁘다.

■ 단원별 문제

| unit 12 감각동사
| unit 13 4형식 동사
| unit 14 문장의 종류

본문 p.146

1. ④
tip! 감각동사 look 다음에는 형용사가 오는데 ④의 sadly는 부사다.
2. ⑤
tip! 보기에 주어진 동사들이 모두 2형식 동사여서 바로 보어인 형용사가 와야 하는데 ⑤의 feel 다음에 온 것은 happily는 부사이다.
3. sweetly → sweet
4. ④
5. Your hand feels cold
6. ⑤
7. ④
tip! buy를 4형식으로 쓰면 '~에게, ~을 사주다'로 해석이 된다.
A: You look happy.
B: Yes I'm so happy, because my mother bought me a computer for my birthday.
A: 너 행복해 보인다.
B: 응 나 정말 행복해, 왜냐하면 부모님이 생일 선물로 컴퓨터를 사주셨거든.
8. to
9. ④
tip! give는 4형식 동사라, 주어와 동사 뒤에 간접목적어(~에게)+직접목적어(~을/를)의 순서로 온다.
10. ⑤
tip! 4형식 문장의 구조이다.
11. ③
tip! 나머지는 모두 4형식 문장이다.
12. ⑤
13. The accident made him strong. (5형식)
14. The plan sounds rational. (2형식)
15. (1) deeply
　　(2) sweet
tip! (1)에 사용된 동사 sleep은 1형식 동사이며,
　　(2)에 사용된 동사 look은 여기서 2형식으로

쓰였다.

16. ①

① She made him sadly. → She made him sad.

17. He cooked bulgogi for me.

18. They showed beautiful pictures to her.

19. The seasoning makes food spicy.

20. buy, make, get, build, cook 등

본문 p.150
Unit 15 to부정사를 목적어로 하는 동사

Exercise 1) 다음 문장에서 어색한 부분을 찾아서 고치세요.

1. save → to save

2. cook → to cook

3. to like → likes

4. quitting → to quit

5. leave → to leave

6. staying → to stay

7. l to decided → l decided

8. drink → to drink

9. to start → start

10. meeting → to meet

Exercise 1-1) 다음 문장에서 어색한 부분을 찾아서 고치세요.

1. to like → like

2. gave → give

3. seeing → see

4. talked → talk

5. dancing → to dance

6. clean → to clean

7. to taking → to take(taking)

8. playing → to play

9. go → to go

10. take → to take

Exercise 2) 다음 문장을 보기의 단어를 활용하여 영작하세요.

1. l hope to visit America.

2. l like to take(taking) a nap.

3. He starts to do(doing) his work.

4. Try to speak in English.

5. l want to wake up early.

6. She likes to dance(dancing) with me.

7. lt starts to rain(raining).

8. Do you want to meet him?

9. l don't like to wear(wearing) this shirt.

10. l am trying to find my watch.

Exercise 2-1) 다음 문장을 보기의 단어를 활용하여 영작하세요.

1. l want to eat something.

2. She tries to speak up.

3. They don't like to clean(cleaning) the window.

4. He hopes to win.

5. We started to eat(eating) fruits.

6. l don't want to leave early.

7. They don't like to stop(stopping) now.

8. She likes to swim(swimming) in the river.

9. Try to think in English.

10. l try to join the team.

본문 p.156
Unit 16 지각동사, 사역동사

Exercise 1) 다음 문장에서 문법적으로 틀린 부분을 고치세요.

1. pass → to pass

2. to play → play(playing)

3. to clean → clean

4. touched → touch(touching)

5. to know → know

6. buy → to buy

7. lying → lie

8. to go → go

9. brought → bring

10. to cry → cry(crying)

Exercise 1-1) 다음 문장에서 문법적으로 틀린 부분을 고치세요.

1. to shout → shout(shouting)
2. to wash → wash
3. played → play(playing)
4. sing → to sing
5. to draw → draw(drawing)
6. left → leave(leaving)
7. to find→ find
8. to sing → sing(singing)
9. doing → do
10. crying → cry

본문 p.158

Exercise 2) 다음 괄호 안의 단어를 이용하여 영작하세요.

1. He wants his son to be a king.
2. He watched her read(reading) the novel.
3. She makes me laugh.
4. We want him to be kind.
5. I had him do his homework.
6. I saw her enter(entering) the room.
7. They felt something stand(standing) behind the back.
8. He heard her sing(singing).
9. She watched me enter(entering) the room.
10. They had me call him.

Exercise 2-1) 다음 괄호 안의 단어를 이용하여 영작하세요.

1. I want him to carry the box.
2. She persuaded him to sell the chair.
3. I saw my son walk(walking).
4. They had him drive.
5. I want you to go to sleep.
6. We forced him to invite her.
7. He felt someone cry(crying).
8. I heard him yell(yelling) at her.
9. She let him read the book.
10. I heard the baby cry(crying).

Unit 17 접속사 that

본문 p.162

Exercise 1) 다음 주어진 문장을 영작하세요.

1. I know that he is handsome.
2. I believe that she is not angry.
3. I think that he is handsome.
4. I hope that she becomes happy.
5. She said that the room was dark.

Exercise 1-1) 다음 주어진 문장을 영작하세요.

1. He knows that she is sad.
2. She believes that he was really busy.
3. I said that he liked her.
4. They thought that he is funny.
5. We hoped that he would come back.

Unit 18 접속사 because, when

본문 p.165

Exercise 1) 빈칸에 because와 when 중 적절한 것을 넣으세요.

1. when / 2. because / 3. because / 4. when / 5. because / 6. when / 7. because / 8. because / 9. because / 10. when

본문 p.166

Exercise 1-1) 빈칸에 because와 when 중 적절한 것을 넣고 해석하세요.

1. when / 2. because / 3. when / 4. because / 5. when / 6. because / 7. because / 8. because / 9. because / 10. because

Exercise 2) 다음 문장을 because나 when을 사용하여 영작하세요.

1. He was tall when he was young.
2. I am hungry now because I didn't have lunch.
3. I cannot buy the car because I am not rich.
4. I can buy the house because I am rich.
5. Please call me when you get home.
6. I was singing in the room when he knocked the door.

7. He plays basketball well because he is tall.
8. She became famous in our town because she is so pretty.
9. I can meet you because I am not busy today.
10. She studied hard when she was in high school.

■ 단원별 문제
| unit 15 to부정사를 목적어로 하는 동사
| unit 16 지각동사, 사역동사
| unit 17 접속사 that
| unit 18 접속사 because, when

본문 p.168

1. ②, ⑤
tip! see는 지각동사이다.
2. ④
3. ⑤
tip! ⑤ She didn't want writing a letter. →
She didn't want to write a letter.
4. ④
5. They like to eat cake.
6. ③
7. ④
8. ④
9. ⑤
10. ①
11. ③, ②
12. I saw him lying on the grass.
13. ⑤
14. ②
15. to go → go
16. ④
17. ②
18. ②
19. ⑤
20. ④
tip! 보기와 ④은 접속사 that이지만 나머지는 전부 지시대명사 that이다.

Unit 19 비교급 및 최상급
본문 p.174
Exercise 1) 다음 주어진 단어의 비교급과 최상급을 만드세요.
1. taller, tallest / 2. hotter, hottest / 3. prettier, prettiest / 4. more famous, most famous / 5. more beautiful, most beautiful

Exercise 1-1) 다음 주어진 단어의 비교급과 최상급을 만드세요.
1. bigger, biggest / 2. shorter, shortest / 3. earlier, earliest / 4. kinder, kindest / 5. more useful, most useful

Exercise 1-2) 다음 주어진 단어의 비교급과 최상급을 만드세요.
1. older(elder), oldest(eldest) / 2. better, best / 3. worse, worst / 4. more, most / 5. cuter, cutest

Exercise 1-3) 다음 주어진 단어의 비교급과 최상급을 만드세요.
1. younger, youngest / 2. more foolish, most foolish / 3. better, best / 4. more, most / 5. worse, worst

본문 p.177
Exercise 1) 다음 문장을 괄호 안의 단어를 참고하여 영작하세요.
1. She is taller than I.
2. He is the tallest in his class.
3. I am older than you.
4. Today is hotter than yesterday.
5. This movie is more interesting than that one.
6. He is stronger than I.
7. This house is bigger than that one.
8. English is more difficult than math.
9. I am happier than you.
10. A pen is more useful than a pencil.

Exercise 1-1) 다음 문장을 괄호 안의 단어를 참고하여 영작하세요.

본문 p.178

1. Your dream is the most important.
2. Mathematics is easier than English.
3. A movie is more interesting than a book.
4. I am wiser than she.
5. This room is larger than that one.
6. Today is warmer than yesterday.
7. He is happier than I.
8. I am younger than you.
9. A car is faster than a bicycle.
10. He is smarter than she.

Exercise 1-2) 다음 문장을 괄호 안의 단어를 참고하여 영작하세요.

1. Jeju island is the largest island in Korea.
2. Love is the most important thing in my life.
3. He is the tallest in his class.
4. She is the youngest in his class.
5. This chair is the most comfortable chair in the world.
6. She is the prettiest of them.
7. This cell phone is the most expensive in the store.
8. Math is the most difficult subject to me.
9. My brother is the strongest man in my family.
10. This box is the biggest box in my house.

Exercise 1-3) 다음 문장을 괄호 안의 단어를 참고하여 영작하세요.

본문 p.180

1. This book is the most interesting book in this library.
2. She is the happiest woman in the world.
3. This room is the largest room in this hotel.
4. This book is the most expensive thing(stuff) in my house.
5. Tom is the tallest boy in my class.
6. Jane is the most beautiful girl in our school.
7. Health is the most important thing in your life.
8. This river is the longest river in the world.
9. The man is the most handsome man in New York.
10. Iron is the most useful of them.

Unit 20 부가의문문

본문 p.183

Exercise 1) 다음 빈칸을 채워 부가의문문을 완성하고 원하는 대답을 하세요.

1. do you / 2. doesn't she / 3. isn't he /
4. won't he / 5. shouldn't we / 6. isn't it /
7. don't you / 8. can't you / 9. doesn't it /
10. do we

Exercise1-1) 다음 빈칸을 채워 부가의문문을 완성하세요.

1. isn't she / 2. aren't they / 3. don't we /
4. don't I / 5. doesn't he / 6. aren't we /
7. do you / 8. does she / 9. can't they /
10. doesn't she

Unit 21 감탄문

본문 p.187

Exercise 1) 다음 문장의 틀린 부분을 옳게 고치세요.

1. What a nice car it is!
2. How beautiful the flower is!
3. How kind the teacher is!
4. What a delicious cake it is!
5. What a handsome man you are!
6. How kind the girl is!
7. What a funny movie it is!
8. What interesting novels they are!
9. How boring this book is!
10. What a tall boy he is!

Exercise 1-1) 다음 문장의 틀린 부분을 옳게 고치세요.

1. What a delicious apple it is!
2. What a nice car it is!
3. What a beautiful picture it is!
4. How gorgeous the room is!
5. What a boring book it is!
6. What a funny drama it is!
7. How gentle the man is!
8. How beautiful the house is!
9. What a nice car it is!
10. What a great pen it is!

■ 단원별 문제

| unit 19 비교급 및 최상급
| unit 20 부가의문문
| unit 21 감탄문

본문 p.189

1. ①
tip! 문장에 than이 있어서 비교급이 필요한데 funny는 비교급이 아니다.

2. ②

3. ③
tip!
① early - earlier - earliest
② long - longer - longest
④ bad - worse - worst
⑤ famous - more famous - most famous

4. ②

5. ④

6. ③
tip! 보기의 문장은 '어떤 강도 나일 강 만큼 길지 않다.'로 원급으로 최상급을 나타낸 것이다.

7. ②

8. ⑤
tip!
① Susan is as tall as Peter.
② It's the fastest animal in the world.
③ You look happier than yesterday.
④ Seoul is one of the oldest cities in the world.

9. ③

10. The cat is dirty, isn't it?

11. ④
tip! ④ don't he → doesn't he

12. ②

13. ③

14. ①, ⑤

15. ④

16. ③

17. will you

18. prettier

19. more popular

20. the biggest

21. what a big

22. How pretty the doll is!

23. ①
tip! ① isn't he → doesn't he

주니어 고릴라 영문법

Junior Gorilla Grammar 1

핵심만 반복, 그리고 영작!

고릴라 영문법 카페에서
추가 자료와 피드백도 받을 수 있습니다.

2,500여 개의 전국 중학교 기출 문제 및 교과서 완전 분석 후 반영
taborm.com과 고릴라 영문법 카페에서 추가 학습 자료 제공